Lesson Planning for Meaningful Variety in Teaching

Lesson Planning for Meaningful Variety in Teaching

Richard M. Henak

Reference & Resource Series

National Education Association
Washington, D.C.

Stock No. 1515-0-00

Note

The opinions expressed in this publication should not be construed as representing the policy or position of the National Education Association. Materials published as part of the Reference & Resource Series are intended to be discussion documents for teachers who are concerned with specialized interests of the profession.

Library of Congress Cataloging in Publication Data

Henak, Richard M.
    Lesson planning for meaningful variety in teaching.

    (Reference & resource series)
    Bibliography: p.
    1. Lesson planning.   I. Title.   II. Series:
Reference and resource series.
LB1027.H396   371.3   79-16197
ISBN 0-8106-1515-0

CONTENTS

ACKNOWLEDGMENTS

Grateful appreciation is due to many who helped to write and prepare this manuscript.

First, my heartfelt appreciation goes to those who developed the sample lesson plans: Ronald Bullock, Roy Connor, Edward Niles, Marty Randall and Michael Tolle. I have been truly blessed with friends who are creative teachers and who are willing to share their talents in this book.

Second, I affectionately thank my wife, Karen, who borders on true genius because of her remarkable skill in converting unintelligible pencil scratching into a beautifully typed manuscript.

My thanks and apologies are also extended to anyone else whose ideas I may have used and to whom I have inadvertently not given credit.

The Author

Richard M. Henak is Professor of Industrial Education and Technology at Ball State University, Muncie, Indiana.

The Consultants

The following educators have reviewed the manuscript and provided helpful comments and suggestions:

Norma Dell Broadway, Instructor and Chairperson, Business and Office Education Department, Hinds Junior College, Jackson Branch, Jackson, Mississippi

Dr. Olive Church, Associate Professor and Program Coordinator, Business Education and Office Administration, Department of Vocational Education, University of Wyoming, Laramie

Catherine M. Clark, Instructor, Gateway Technical Institute, Kenosha, Wisconsin

Dr. Robert R. Hanson, Associate Professor, Department of Vocational-Technical Education, University of Tennessee, Knoxville

Dr. Luther E. Judt, Chairperson, Teacher Education, Red River Community College, Winnipeg, Manitoba, Canada.

INTRODUCTION

WHY THIS BOOK?

In developing a course, the teacher strives to identify goals that are appropriate to the learner, to select an effective sequence for presentations, and to make numerous other decisions that will result in a high-quality learning experience. These preliminary steps are essential but are of little value if a variety of interesting, relevant, and efficient teaching/learning (T/L) techniques are not used in the daily lessons. To improve education, teachers must improve daily lessons. Large budgets, modern buildings, and better trained teachers, although important, contribute little to the education of youth until effective daily lessons are conducted.

Lesson Planning for Meaningful Variety in Teaching was written to help teachers improve the effectiveness of daily lessons. The effort expended to write this book was motivated by the belief that conducting a variety of interesting and effective lessons is a learnable and valuable skill for all interested teachers.

Providing variety in teaching is relatively easy. All the teacher must do is to accumulate the knowledge and skill necessary to implement a wide range of T/L techniques and then to use the techniques randomly. Meaningful variety is maximized only when two sets of conditions occur. First, the teacher must be familiar with the learner, objectives, school environment, many T/L techniques, guidelines for selecting T/L techniques, and ways of varying the classroom environment. Second, the teacher must be flexible enough to use such knowledge and skill to respond to the multitude of complexities that occur throughout the school day.

WHAT IS MEANINGFUL VARIETY?

Meaningful variety is a phenomenon that can be described by using a continuum. At one end no variety is used; at the other end the maximum meaningful variety is provided. Most teachers probably function somewhere in between the two extremes. Six descriptions of teaching behavior are given to illustrate different levels of the use of meaningful variety. Figure 1 is included to assist in visualizing the concept.

Figure 1.
MEANINGFUL VARIETY SCALE

The teacher who enters the classroom everyday when the bell rings, reads the lecture, stops when the bell rings at the end of the period, and then leaves the room would be placed at location "A" on the continuum.

The teacher who is similar to "A" but who uses stimulus variation in the lecture by moving about the room, shifting sensory channels, employing pauses, gestures, and voice intonations would fit into position "B."

By randomly varying T/L techniques, teacher "C" adds variety to classroom activities which may possibly result in an increased level of interest and effectiveness simply because of the reduced monotony and because the "shotgun" approach increases the probability of matching an effective T/L technique with the learning styles of a number of students.

In the next case, teacher "D" uses a variety of T/L techniques but matches them with the intended instructional outcomes. This teacher provides variety with greater meaning by applying another generally accepted principle of learning: We learn what we do.

Teacher "E" provides more meaningful variety because T/L techniques are matched with students' preferred learning styles (e.g., reading, listening, or doing) as well as with the intended instructional outcomes. As more and more conditions of learning are considered, the more meaningful the variety and the more effective the instruction.

Finally, teacher "F" provides an opportunity for students to select the objectives and the appropriate learning strategies to achieve them. At this stage the variety of T/L techniques has the potential for being the most meaningful of all the illustrations.

THE ANALOGY

In an effort to help you understand how to put meaningful variety into your teaching, an analogy is made between the performance of the successful furniture builder and the performance of the teacher. *Materials* used by the furniture builder may be compared to the teacher's *students* and *course objectives.*

Next, the drawings and written details used to describe the *specifications* of a piece of furniture may be compared to the *performance objectives* used to specify instructional intent.

Third, the furniture builder's *tools* may be compared to the teacher's *T/L techniques.* Where furniture builders use saws, drills, and planers, teachers use lectures, experiments, and discussions.

Quality furniture is seldom the result of haphazard efforts randomly or impulsively expended. It requires production *planning* that is directed toward producing skillfully made pieces that match the specifications. Teaching is similar. Purposeful planning is directed toward reaching the performance objectives that describe the intended outcomes of instruction. *Lessons* are the vehicle to achieve objectives and *lesson plans* are descriptions of that vehicle.

Selecting the right tools for use in a furniture-making operation is essential if high-quality work is to be produced in a reasonable length of time. *Selecting the best T/L techniques* for the situation is equally important for teachers but far more difficult than selecting woodworking tools.

Finally, to produce furniture that meets specifications and to do so efficiently requires efficient *working conditions,* including decisions as to the person who specifies the product (builder or customer) and the size of the work force to be employed to produce the piece of furniture. Similar decisions concerning *learning conditions* need to be made by teachers; for example, the person who identifies the objectives (teacher or student), the size of the work groups, and the kind of competitive/cooperative environment to be established. These are some of the concerns of this book.

HOW TO USE THE BOOK

The best way to use this book is to read it from beginning to end. Then, go back and review each chapter in the context of a familiar T/L situation. The material on planning presentation, action, and interaction techniques will be most useful if lessons are planned and implemented using each technique. After competency is developed in the use of these techniques, attempt to implement a different class organization, degree of teacher/student dominance, and goal structure. Be cautious, do not attempt too much at once.

If you are familiar with any of the methods given, scan them or pass over them entirely and turn to those which may be unfamiliar. Read them and apply their suggestions.

The secret of getting the most benefit from this book is to read it and *adapt and apply the ideas to a particular situation.* Work with these ideas and use them. The more you do so, the greater the benefit to you and your students.

Chapter 1.

WHY PUT MEANINGFUL VARIETY INTO LESSONS?
(Understanding the Materials)

Purpose: Builders of fine furniture are familiar with the materials of the trade. They can inspect the materials closely. They know about the characteristics of the materials and how they are affected by environmental conditions. They know how to use the most appropriate tools and processes in forming the product to the specifications. In each of the worker's decisions an effort is made to enhance the strong points and to minimize the weaknesses of the materials. This chapter will help you to understand variations in students and in instructional outcomes (the materials of education). These materials are also affected by administrative conditions that must be responded to if effective instruction is to occur.

Objective: When you have completed this chapter, you will understand three educational variables (i.e., learner characteristics, intended outcomes, and administrative conditions) well enough to write or state a rationale for putting meaningful variety into lesson plans.

The reasons for using a variety of classroom activities are far more complex than simply trying to entertain students. Teaching/learning (T/L) techniques are educational tools that are selected in response to conditions that affect learning. The value of providing meaningful variety is found in trying to match T/L methodology with the inherent variations that occur in students, the intended outcomes from instruction, and the administrative conditions that occur in schools.

STUDENT VARIABLES

Students must be the central focus in education. Schools exist for them. Unless students learn in schools, there is no purpose for schools to exist. When students do not learn, it may be because they, rather than the subject matter, are misunderstood. One does not have to visit a classroom long before discovering that within any group of students there is great variation in individual educational, intellectual, emotional, social, and physical characteristics. There is no typical student; each one is a unique combination of many qualities.

1. *Educational Characteristics*

Variations in educational characteristics include differences in student achievement levels in the basic skills of reading, computing, writing, and other relevant areas of instruction. Information relative to the educational characteristics of individual students may be obtained by reviewing records of significant experiences, course records, administrative records, or preassessment instruments, as well as by teacher observations, interviews, and assessments. When information about each student's educational development is known, instructional sequences, vocabulary, drill sessions, projects, examples, and instructional materials are more easily selected.

2. *Intellectual Characteristics*

Essentially, intellectual characteristics may be categorized into two areas—variations in learning potential and in learning style.

a. Learning Potential

Variations in learning potential involve the rate, quantity, and levels of objectives that students have the ability to learn. These variables are often measured with IQ tests and other mental aptitude measures; they may also be determined by teacher assessment and observation. Decisions relevant to levels of expectations, pacing, kinds of practice, and amounts of practice are based upon this information.

b. Learning Style

The effect of learning styles on learning has received a great deal of attention in recent years. Unique to each student, learning styles consist of the conditions under which the student prefers to learn as well as the sensory modality preferred. The conditions of learning include such variations as fast paced/leisurely paced, quiet background/noisy background, easy work/challenging work, individual activities/group activities, and formal classroom structure/informal classroom structure.

The second consideration in learning styles is the student's preferred learning mode. Most material is learned through the visual mode (seeing), the auditory mode (hearing), and the action mode (doing). After the teacher has identified the learning styles that are most successful with each student, activities may be chosen and used to strengthen the student's ability. When the student has learned successfully with a particular style, alternate techniques may be introduced and tried so that new styles may be developed to correct weaknesses. For example, a student who learns well by doing may experience problems and waste time trying to install a tape player and speakers in an automobile without reading the instructions. The teacher can help the student develop the learning-by-doing style, but may also provide encouragement to read instructions first. The latter technique may be faster and less risky.

3. Emotional and Social Characteristics

Emotional characteristics vary greatly from student to student, from day to day, and from hour to hour. The most effective teacher will have the greatest number of T/L techniques from which to choose, the skill in making good selections, and the flexibility to change techniques when particular students experience difficulty.

Perceptive teachers can identify interest and attitude characteristics by means of student conferences and interviews, in-class and out-of-class discussions, pupil autobiographies, questionnaires, and values clarification activities. Because of the great diversity in any classroom group, the more systematic the teacher can be in obtaining pertinent information and in responding to it, the greater the possibility of success in helping the student to make positive growth as a result of involvement in school activities.

Students also vary in social growth in such areas of interpersonal skills as cooperation, adaptability, leadership, dependability, and initiative. Sociograms, "guess-who" charts, social distance charts, and perceptive observations are useful sources of data on the social development of the students in a classroom group.

4. Physical Characteristics

Finally, instruction can be more meaningful if the selection of T/L techniques is responsive to the physical characteristics of students. Some students may have sensory handicaps in seeing, hearing, and perceptual-motor skills. So-called normal students may also vary in numerous ways—in physical speed, endurance, strength, reaction time, appearance, size, and maturity, to list only a few. Teaching/learning techniques should therefore be designed to help develop the necessary physical characteristics and utilize them in a positive manner, without exceeding the student's capability.

When teachers are aware of these differences, they can select appropriate approaches to introduce, demonstrate, and practice physical development skills. Many cognitive and affective behaviors may also be reinforced by using the physical "doing" activities. With such techniques students experience abstract phenomena or confirm the abstractions through more than one sense modality.

Obviously, the matching of student characteristics and T/L techniques is difficult. When it is done well, however, instruction will be more effective. Continuous efforts should therefore be made to find student strengths and to capitalize on them.

INTENDED OUTCOMES

Intended outcomes, the planned behavioral changes which result from an organized module of instruction, fall within three domains—cognitive (thinking), psychomotor (physically doing), and affective (feeling). According to various authors, descriptions of teaching are subdivided into three or more levels. In developing competencies in any of the three domains, students should, in most cases, (1) receive information about the behavior, (2) experience the behavior, and (3) practice the behavior. No single technique is adequate to communicate all three steps. Teachers must have a large collection of T/L techniques from which to choose and considerable skill in selecting and using them in order to *effectively* help students develop competencies in the various levels of the three domains.

ADMINISTRATIVE CONDITIONS

Although the number and magnitude of administrative variables differ from day to day and from school to school, in all schools teachers must compensate for them from time to time. These variables may include the following:

- Time of day

- Class or school events preceding or following the class
- Size of class
- Student responsibilities (family or work) after school
- Elective or required class.

All these factors must be considered in the teacher's decision as to what will take place in the classroom during class time.

SUMMARY

Students vary greatly. Their individual interpretation of what occurs in the classroom is determined by many variables, including the following:

- Ability to assimilate new information with what is already known
- Intellectual capability to receive the information as it is presented
- Interest in the information
- Adaptability of the new information to the physical development of the student.

The teacher's ability to perceptively analyze the students in the classroom will determine, in a large measure, the success of the instruction.

Chapter 2.

DESCRIBING INSTRUCTIONAL INTENT
(Writing Specifications)

Purpose: Some successful artisans create with materials with no visible prior plan in mind. They let the variations in the material determine the shape and character of the piece they build. There are also some truly artistic teachers who do not appear to have an objective, but who are able to successfully follow the students' interests, thoughts, and abilities and guide them to achieve lofty heights. Most successful teachers, however, conduct T/L activities with objectives clearly in mind, just as most skilled designer/builders work from sketches or drawings prepared by themselves or others. Work does not begin until all the details are clear to the builder. It is recommended that the intent for each module of instruction be specified by performance objectives which are clearly understood and recorded before teaching begins. This chapter provides an opportunity to learn how to analyze instructional intent and to describe it in a performance objective.

Objective: When you have completed this chapter, you will understand it well enough to enable you to—

1. Analyze a cognitive, psychomotor, or affective behavior in terms of domain and levels within the domain.

2. State an intended instructional outcome in a student-oriented performance objective that includes the important conditions, observable behavior, and level of performance.

WHAT ARE INTENDED OUTCOMES?

Intended outcomes are planned cognitive, affective, and psychomotor changes in a learner as a result of instruction.

A good way to start is to identify some key words in the definition. Notice the inclusion of *planned*. Unexpected outcomes of instruction may occur. Since they are not planned, it is hard to control their occurrence. If they are positive outcomes, try to have them occur again; if they are negative, however, try to prevent them from happening a second time.

Next in the definition are three kinds of modifications—cognitive, affective, and psychomotor. The *cognitive* domain consists of the intellectual responses made by the learner. Such responses may include estimating construction costs, writing essay tests, and solving engineering problems in drafting. The *affective* domain involves the attitudinal, emotional, and valuing responses made by the learner, usually classified as interests, attitudes, and appreciations. The *psychomotor* domain consists of physical responses made by the learner, as in the skilled use of tools and materials and in improved performances in sports.

Figure 2 summarizes the levels within each domain from lowest to highest. More detailed information, including examples for each domain and sample action verbs to describe behaviors, may be found in three works cited in the Selected References (Bloom for the cognitive domain, Krathwohl for the affective domain, and Hauenstein for the psychomotor domain).

Cognitive Domain	Affective Domain	Psychomotor Domain
1. Knowledge 2. Comprehension 3. Application 4. Analysis 5. Synthesis 6. Evaluation	1. Receiving 2. Responding 3. Valuing 4. Organizing 5. Characterizing	1. Perceiving 2. Imitating 3. Manipulating 4. Performing 5. Perfecting

Figure 2.

LEVELS WITHIN DOMAINS OF TAXONOMIES OF EDUCATIONAL OBJECTIVES

The three domains and the levels within each are easily understood. What may not be apparent is that a particular human behavior is not exclusively a cognitive, affective, or psychomotor function but a combination of all three domains. For example, safe and skillful operation of a machine lathe is classified as a psychomotor performance but it involves, among other things, cognitive knowledge about what is safe—the safety rules. Furthermore, working safely and carefully goes beyond physical ability and knowledge. It also includes an attitude—*will* the operator do what is known to be right and what can be performed physically?

The person who has a well-defined, consistent, and clear value system is performing at the upper levels of the affective domain. To achieve this level of performance, both knowledge of the possible consequences of the alternatives and the physical ability to communicate with others are needed to test the value system. The cognitive and the psychomotor skills thus support the affective behavior.

Even writing a paper and pencil essay test, which is considered a cognitive process, requires the physical movement of the pencil and the possession of a cooperative attitude to complete the test, thereby combining all three domains.

Clearly, then, *no domain operates alone.* Even so, there is an advantage in thinking of outcomes in terms of being primarily in one dominant area. Once the teacher is aware of the domain that is dominant, it is easier to select the effective instructional technique to develop the intended outcome. Psychomotor skills are efficiently learned from demonstrations and practice, less efficiently learned from lectures and reading alone. When attempting to develop positive attitudes toward safety or a subject matter area, modeling and role-playing are more effective than lecturing. But when it comes to knowledge, particularly in the lower levels in the taxonomy, lecture, programmed instruction, and reading may very well be superior to demonstrations and role-playing.

In summary, the intended outcomes are the "stuff" the student learns—cognitive stuff such as stating the safety margin for a jointer; psychomotor stuff such as the ability to joint a narrow board on a jointer without getting a hand inside the safety margin; affective stuff such as voluntarily practicing good safety habits while operating potentially dangerous equipment.

SPECIFYING INTENDED OUTCOMES

For years teachers have been told to develop objectives. Despite the attention given objectives in the past, however, few teachers derived many instructional dividends from expressing their goals, mainly becuase they were stated in terms too imprecise to be effective. Since the early 1960s, a development of major significance has been under way regarding the statement of instructional goals. Educators have been urged since that time to describe their objectives in terms of measurable behavior. In the writer's view, this is one of the most important advances in education in the twentieth century and one which has launched a significant attack upon the problems of education. Precise objectives are the basis of this book's point of view.

It may be helpful, at this point, to clarify some terminology. Several authors have made distinctions between the terms *behavioral objectives, instructional objectives, performance objectives, specific objectives,* and perhaps others. For present purposes, no distinctions are made between these terms.

The purpose of an instructional objective is to communicate to students, teachers, and other interested persons what the student may expect to learn from a module of instruction. The statement includes a clear description of the observable behavior, the conditions under which the behavior will occur, and a measurable level of quality for the performance.

Once the observable behavior is clearly defined, it is easier to select T/L techniques that will be successful in introducing students to the concept, skill, or attitude, and to provide them with opportunities to practice the behavior.

When the conditions are clear, students and teacher know what relevant references, time, equipment, information, and materials will be available in support of the students as they progress through the learning activities.

Finally, if the level of performance is stated, students will know when an objective is accomplished or why it was not accomplished. Then the teacher has a criterion that is useful in evaluating and reporting student progress.

Some distinctions need to be made between objectives used to describe the intended outcomes from different curricular levels. The four objectives that follow are stated in performance terms, but the degree of generality expressed in the conditions, observable behavior, and level of performance varies. The following is an example of a *program objective*.

Upon completing the program's required industrial arts courses, the student will be able to use technical graphics to clearly communicate shapes, sizes, quantities, qualities, conditions, and conceptual information.

—Conditions:	Upon completing the required industrial arts courses . . .
—Observable Behavior:	. . . use technical graphics to clearly communicate shapes, sizes, quantities, qualities, conditions, and conceptual information . . .
—Level of Performance:	. . . clearly . . .

In the following *course objective* each component becomes more specific.

Upon completing the course in technical graphics, the student will be able to make charts and graphs, isometric, orthographic, one- and two-

point perspectives, pattern and schematic sketches that are accurate, complete, and neatly done.

—Conditions:	Upon completing the technical graphics course . . .
—Observable Behavior:	. . . make charts and graphs, isometric, orthographic, one- and two-point perspectives, pattern and schematic sketches . . .
—Level of Performance:	. . . accurate, complete, and neatly done.

A *unit objective* describes a smaller segment of instruction and is even more precise, as in the following example.

Upon completing the unit on charts, graphs, and diagrams, and when given quantitative and conceptual information, the student will be able to design and sketch a chart or graph to communicate the quantitative data, and a diagram to communicate the conceptual information that is efficient, legible, well proportioned, and accurate.

From the previous examples, it should now be possible to identify the components of the objective. Try to do so. Then check your attempt with the following interpretation.

—Conditions:	Upon completing the unit on charts, graphs, and diagrams, and when given quantitative and conceptual information . . .
—Observable Behavior:	. . . design and sketch a chart or graph to communicate the quantitative data, and a diagram to communicate the conceptual information . . .
—Level of Performance:	. . . efficient, legible, well proportioned, and accurate.

Finally, the *lesson* is the most specific level for which performance objectives are prepared. Try to identify each component in the objective that follows.

At the end of the lesson, and when given the number of base hits made by a fictitious baseball player in each of ten games, as well as a sheet of graph paper and a pencil, the student will be able to design and sketch a line graph that has the variable quantity and the fixed-increment data on the correct axes, accuracy, uniform and legible lettering, and correctly spelled and capitalized words.

The following components should have been indicated:

—*Conditions:* At the end of the lesson, and when given the number of base hits made by a fictitious baseball player in each of ten games, as well as a sheet of graph paper and a pencil . . .

—*Observable Behavior:* . . . design and sketch a line graph . . .

—*Level of Performance:* . . . has the variable quantity and the fixed-increment data on the correct axes, accuracy, uniform and legible lettering, and correctly spelled and capitalized words.

A review of these objectives demonstrates that each of the components becomes more and more specific as the module of instruction becomes more and more specific.

If you are unskilled in writing performance objectives, practice will be helpful. Use your subject matter area as a reference and try to write objectives for each level—program, course, unit, and lesson.

An aid to writing performance objectives that has proven successful for others and that may be helpful is illustrated in Figure 3. The headings may be duplicated on a 3 x 5 inch format and a number of sheets bound into a note pad, or separate sheets may be used.

By using each of the three areas given in the aid, you are certain to include all components. Each component may be changed, as necessary, rewriting the entire objective. Some of the following suggestions may also be of assistance:

Conditions:

Observable Behavior:

Level of Performance:

Figure 3.
AID FOR WRITING PERFORMANCE OBJECTIVES

—*Conditions:* Amount of time or space; available equipment, materials, tools, and information; deadline dates or times; number and kinds of available references, if any.

—*Observable Behaviors:* Be sure that this component describes something the student does that can be seen.

—*Level of Performance:* Percentage correct; expected number correct from the number possible; descriptions of grammatical quality; plus or minus accuracy of sizes or computations; neatness; number of variables included in answer of essay questions.

When the objectives have been completed, they should be carefully checked. Then a colleague may be asked to review them. Look for the following points:

- Are the objectives clear and concise?
- Are the objectives realistic for the grade level?
- Are the objectives attainable by instruction?
- Are the objectives capable of being measured?
- Are the relevant conditions included?

- Is the student behavior stated in observable terms?
- Is the level of performance stated?

SUMMARY

Once the skill of specifying the intended outcomes has been developed, it will be easier to communicate the instructional intent of the module to interested people, to select more appropriate T/L techniques, and to evaluate student progress as well as the effectiveness of specific instruction.

Chapter 3.

THE KINDS OF T/L TECHNIQUES
(Identifying the Tools)

Purpose: Skilled woodworkers must be knowledgeable about and skilled in the use of a wide variety of tools and machines. The kind of product that can be built is greatly limited if the woodworker is able to use only a saw, a drill, and a planer. Teachers are also limited when they can use only two or three T/L techniques in their teaching. This chapter introduces a range of T/L techniques that can be learned and used by skilled teachers to help students achieve a wide range of goals.

Objective: When you have completed this chapter, you will know enough about T/L techniques to enable you to—

1. Distinguish between the three categories of T/L techniques.

2. Find a detailed description, planning guidelines, and examples of recommended lesson plans using each technique.

Today's teachers have a multitude of T/L techniques from which to choose. The techniques to be discussed have been grouped into three categories—*presentations, actions,* and *interactions.* The key distinction between the categories is the role students play in the implementation of the T/L techniques. In presentations, students are relatively inactive or passive. In the action techniques, however, students are actively engaged in manipulating ideas, materials, and tools. In interaction techniques, students are also active but, in this case, they are active in interpersonal exchanges of ideas and feelings.

These three categories were selected because of their resemblance to the ways we interact with our environment outside school. We learn in natural conditions by observing (listening, watching, and feeling), by interacting with things (building, experimenting, and examining), or by interacting with people (visiting, interviewing, and discussing). Teaching/learning activities in school can utilize these same modes of learning.

PRESENTATION TECHNIQUES

Presentation techniques are most often selected to provide classroom management information (e.g., descriptions of assignments, clean-up procedures, policies, schedules of activities, rules for student behavior) and subject matter information (e.g., procedures for investigating a subject, facts, guidelines, interpretations, generalizations, and principles). Chapter 6 discusses the characteristics, uses, planning procedures, and evaluation of these techniques, including three types of lectures and demonstrations, an audiovisual presentation, and a field trip.

ACTION TECHNIQUES

Action techniques directly involve the learner with ideas, materials, objects, and equipment. Students experiment, construct, observe, and otherwise manipulate their body and objects in an effort to—

- Practice a skill, procedure, or process.
- Observe phenomena in concrete form.
- Understand an abstract principle in greater depth.
- Transfer a principle, skill, or process to a new situation.

Chapter 7 discusses three kinds of projects, an expercise, an experiment, and a guided observation technique, together with a description and an example of each.

INTERACTION TECHNIQUES

Interaction techniques capitalize on the human desire to talk and share one's thoughts. Personal interaction is an activity in which two or more people contribute and exchange their ideas. A major advantage of these techniques is that students and their ideas and efforts become the resources and are thus major elements of the T/L environment.

Ten interaction techniques are presented in Chapter 8: questioning, discussions, buzz sessions, brainstorming, seminars, interviewing, role-playing, gaming, committees, and debates.

The outline that follows includes all the T/L techniques to be discussed. Page numbers are given where detailed descriptions of each technique may be found. Sample lessons appear in the Appendix.

SUMMARY

Teaching/learning techniques are the tools of teaching. To teach creatively, multiple options must be available to the teacher. The twenty-four T/L techniques listed are discussed in detail in subsequent chapters. There is much to learn about their use in more classroom situations. The better your knowledge and understanding of these tools, the more creative your teaching will be.

Chapter 4.

PLANNING LESSONS
(Planning Production)

Purpose: A piece of high-quality furniture does not just happen. Its production is the result of an understanding of the specifications, of the avaiability of materials and equipment, and of carefully made production plans. This chapter provides guidelines and suggestions for making lesson plans that lead to accomplishing instructional objectives.

Objective: When you have completed this chapter, you will understand enough about the elements of a lesson and a lesson plan form to enable you to—

1. Distinguish verbally and from memory in two or more ways between a lesson and a lesson plan.
2. State verbally the three major components of a lesson and include one illustration of each.
3. State verbally six to eight elements normally found in a lesson plan.

LESSON COMPONENTS

The outline and objectives provide the course skeleton, but the lessons are the flesh of instruction. A lesson is usually one or two days' learning experiences related to one objective, and it is managed by the teacher. The teacher may plan, organize, and lead activities or may provide an opportunity for learners to do much of the planning, organizing, and leading. Whoever conducts the management functions is dependent upon such variables as the teacher's philosophy of education, the course objectives, the nature of the students, student objectives, and the type of course. Regardless of who manages the activities, lessons play a key role in carrying out a module of instruction.

There are as many ways of describing lesson components as there are authors writing about them. The description selected here, which is a synthesis from several authors, includes three elements that should be included in most, if not all, lessons.

1. *Orientation*

The orientation is designed to motivate the learner to engage in the T/L activities. Three typical functions are the following:

a. *Understanding the purpose*

Students whill engage in activities if they feel that what they are learning is of value. Several techniques can be employed to achieve this feeling of value.

One of the most used and probably the least effective technique is *exhortation*: "You should learn this material because it is good for you," or "This information will be useful to you in later life." If the student values the teacher's opinion, an occasional use of exhortation may be effective, but repeated use of the technique will result in little, if any, motivational effect.

Extrinsic rewards such as grades, recognition, or praise usually help to motivate students and are especially useful in prompting learners to make initial responses. Generally such techniques should be used sparingly, however, because they usually produce short-term results. Involvement in the learning activity may stop when the rewards stop.

A *deductive approach* is employed when the teacher describes practical ways in which learners can use the understanding, skill, or attitude. This technique not only helps students understand why the objective is of value, it also helps the teacher select activities to which students can relate more closely.

The *intrinsic approach* is the most difficult but probably the most effective when used with brighter or more mature learners. To implement this technique questions or situations are devised to stimulate curiosity about the principles, skills, topics, or procedures to be learned. A question such as "What do you think about having a nuclear-powered generating plant built on the south side of town?" may be used to introduce a unit or an activity dealing with the generation of electricity using nuclear energy.

Any of the four techniques described can help to answer the question "Why should I spend my time doing what the teacher has planned?" This function is best served when the purpose is stated early in the instruction and is repeated periodically thereafter.

b. Tie-in

A second function of the orientation is to clarify how the new learning activities fit into the preceding or following experiences. This function is especially necessary if the new activities appear to be unrelated or if the past experiences were complex and students are having difficulty sorting out the essential understandings. Such sentences as "Remember when we developed and sequenced the manufacturing processes? We will now use that sequence in designing our plant layout" should help tie together class activities and orientate students to the lesson.

c. Stating the aim

Several studies suggest that revealing the objective or aim assists learners in reaching the objective.

Stating the aim helps students focus their energies on tasks relevant to it.

2. Development

The development portion of the lesson includes the implementation of the T/L technique(s) that have been selected to help learners achieve the objective. This is the time when the teacher leads the activities and students carry them out. What actually occurs is as diverse as the teacher's knowledge of T/L techniques and the teacher's creativity in their implementation. Although this element is diverse, it should consist of two kinds of activities: (1) the *presentation* by lectures, demonstrations, audiovisuals, or field trips; and (2) the *application* by exercises, discussions, group work, projects, assignments, or other T/L techniques.

In the *presentation* portion of the lesson, two kinds of information are conveyed. Management information acquaints students with procedures concerning carrying out an activity, classroom or school policies, and schedules for test days and deadlines. Such communications are not directly related to the subject matter but to the conduct of school and class activities.

Subject matter information is directly related to the lesson objectives. It is conveyed when the teacher or other presenter tells and/or shows students about relevant principles, concepts, relationships, facts, and feelings.

When a cognitive objective is the focus of the lesson, lectures of all kinds, demonstrations of principles, and audiovisual presentations may be used effectively. If a psychomotor objective is the target, demonstrations and how-to audiovisual presentations are often used. In the case of affective objectives, presentations are often directed toward setting the stage for an interaction activity. Relevant information is thus provided before students become involved in role-playing, discussions, games, interviews, or other interaction techniques.

The *application* portion of the lesson provides students with an opportunity to practice or perform the behavior described in the objective. Application activities cover the range of action and interaction techniques. If the objective is cognitive, students may discuss a topic, play a drill game, conduct an experiment, or become involved in one of many other techniques which help them to use the new understanding.

Application activities that lead to achieving a psychomotor objective may include a project, exercise, or experiment. These T/L techniques offer the student an occasion to practice the skill demonstrated in the presentation portion of the lesson.

Activities designed to apply affective behaviors might include role-playing and discussions. Role-playing requires that the student act out the feelings of others; discussions can bring out the logical consequnces of a variety of decisions and points of view.

3. *Follow-up*

Follow-up activities provide opportunities to obtain closure on an idea by solidifying the concept, building greater understanding or skill, and transferring knowledge from classroom use to life situations. They may include summaries, assignments, and evaluations.

a. *Summaries*

The summary is used sometimes during the development of a lesson and should always occur at the end. It pulls together the happenings in the lesson and relates them to the objectives. Several useful functions can be served by this follow-up activity.

Summaries can help students *correlate* data. Following an experiment with a variety of adhesives, students can correlate the effect of heat, moisture, and time with the strength of the joints.

The teacher can *crystallize a concept* in a summary following a discussion on safety programs by asking for illustrations of each component of the program.

Use of the *"springboard" function* sets the stage for future activities, as, for example, in a social studies class, the statement: "Now that we have learned about several events that contributed to the settling of the West, we can identify individual projects that will help us understand them more fully."

The summary is useful in *developing transfer knowledge*. The following question will help students apply to new situations what they have learned about economics: "On the basis of what we have learned about the concept of supply and demand in determining the cost of gasoline, how would you explain the variations in the prices of produce in the supermarket?"

b. *Assignments*

As a follow-up activity, an assignment is specific work to be done by the student outside of class time for the next class meeting or a future class. Assignments may be used to *reinforce* the classroom T/L activity. When studying pollution of the environment, for example, students might visit an industrial firm, interview an environmental engineer, prepare a report on a company's efforts to protect the environment, or do any one of a multitude of other pertinent activities to reinforce what has been learned in class.

Take-home projects like sculpturing, drawing, and typing are useful in psychomotor *skill development activities*. Written assignments and drill problems aid students in developing cognitive skills. Affective objectives at the lower levels may be developed by student interviews of people who possess the attitudes that are the focus of instruction. Higher level affective objectives may be achieved when students try out new positive attitudes in life situations.

A *preparation assignment* is one in which the student acquires in a prescribed way or in a self-directed way the knowledge needed for future use in a discussion, debate, competitive game, or oral report. Such assignments may be in the form of reading, viewing a television program, or observing specific audiovisual materials.

c. *Evaluation*

Evaluation activities may include specific questioning, short paper/pencil tests, example problems administered at the end of the lesson; in addition to teacher observation and assessment of student performances and works, peer evaluation, and self-evaluation. Through these methods, teachers can determine whether or not to go forward with the lesson; they can also identify students having difficulty as well as specific areas where review may be necessary.

When lessons carry over to a second day, evaluations may be used to assess the day's activities and to set goals for the next day.

LESSON PLANS

The tangible product developed as a result of specifying a lesson is the lesson plan. Lesson plans are to the teacher what drawings, specifications, and bills of material are to the furniture builder. They should be complete enough so that any qualified person can teach from them. They should not be too brief. They should include a systematic form and all important components. There are several practical reasons for including certain details in lesson plans.

- *Improvement of preparation.* The lesson plan provides a well-thoughtout, detailed plan for conducting a class.

- *Economy of time.* If a lesson is taught two to four times a year, details need not be recalled each time. With a plan, the information is available and ready to be adapted to the current situation.

- *Facilitation of improvement.* If there is no record of a previous lesson, it is difficult to remember what occurred and to make course improvements. The lesson plan can help.

- *Ease in ordering supplies.* The materials list on the lesson plan facilitates requisitioning equipment and materials.

- *Guide for substitute teacher.* Lesson plans enable the substitute teacher to carry on the regular class activities. Without them, the substitute may be able only to "babysit."

- *Protection against liability.* If the teacher can offer proof that safety procedures are taught in certain classes, it is more difficult to show negligence on the teacher's part. A lesson plan which includes safety content is one way to help establish such proof. For example, science teachers would include safety rules related to heating liquids in test tubes. Among the many possible precautions that might be listed are the following: heat the test tube evenly by keeping it moving over the flame; point the test tube away from others; avoid breathing fumes; and put the test tube in a holder.

Although the importance of lesson plans is great, their format is not. Most authors include a lesson *title* that describes what the student is to learn. The observable behavior stated in the objective should provide some direction for its selection.

The *objective* is an accurate description of "what" the learner is to be able to do, "how well" it is to be done, and under what conditions it is to be done. The more clearly the teacher understands the objective, the easier to select the T/L technique.

A *list of equipment and materials* needed by teacher and students to carry out the lesson is useful in saving planning time, in reducing the chances of forgetting an essential item, and in ordering supplies for the future. The list should include each item of equipment or material used by teacher and students.

The specific entries in the *content and procedures* are descriptions of the teacher activities in the lesson. The elements of orientation, development, and follow-up described earlier should be included. The development consists of phrases in outline form and in sequential order, descriptions of all managerial instructions, and the subject matter content to be presented students.

The Appendix contains a lesson plan format that has been used successfully for several years. This plan may be adopted or adapted, or another may be selected that better fits individual needs or preferences.

The following summary outline may help to crystallize the contents of this chapter.

A. **Lesson Components**

  1. Orientation
     a. Understanding the purpose
        —Exhortation
        —Extrinsic rewards
        —Deductive approach

—Intrinsic approach
   b. Tie-in
   c. Stating the aim
2. Development
   a. Presentation
   b. Application
3. Follow-up
   a. Summaries
     —Correlate data
     —Crystallize a concept
     —"Springboard"
     —Develop transfer knowledge
   b. Assignments
   c. Evaluations

B. Lesson Plans

1. Title
2. Objective
3. Equipment
   a. Teacher
   b. Student
4. Materials
   a. Teacher
   b. Student
5. Content and Procedures
   a. Orientation
   b. Development
   c. Follow-up

Chapter 5.

SELECTING T/L TECHNIQUES
(Choosing the Right Tool for the Job)

Purpose: In building fine furniture, the specifications call for a number of changes to be made in the material—sawing, planing, drilling, smoothing, shaping, and assembling, to mention only a few. One tool or operation is not capable of making all these changes (e.g., saws will not drill holes). As the woodworker must be able to select the tool best suited to make the desired change in the material, so the teacher must select the most efficient T/L technique to facilitate the behavioral change specified in the objective. In teaching, no single technique is capable of producing all the changes called for in a list of objectives. This chapter offers some guidelines to assist in the selection of the appropriate techniques.

Objective: When you have completed this chapter, you will better understand the process so that you can use the guidelines to select appropriate T/L techniques to achieve state objectives.

PLANNING LESSONS

There are many techniques for presenting information, transmitting skills, and developing attitudes. Since all are not equally effective in reaching each instructional goal, it will be useful to discuss the basis upon which intelligent choices may be made. A word of caution is in order, however. Although schools and instructors have been in existence for centuries and educational researchers have been at work for decades, there is as yet no scientifically based guide for making an accurate selection of appropriate instructional strategies. Psychological research has, of course, provided some insight. In this chapter, an attempt is made to translate such information into usable guides for the selection of instructional procedures and materials.

Among the variables that influence lesson planning are instructional objectives, techniques, external conditions, and selection guidelines. The better each variable is understood, the greater the probability of making sound tactical decisions. Instructional objectives are discussed in Chapter 2; techniques are described briefly in Chapter 3. External conditions and selection guidelines are discussed here.

EXTERNAL CONDITIONS

The problems of external forces are so particularized that little would be gained by studying them out of context. Therefore, only a superficial coverage follows. Teachers must function in a context which exerts a number of forces requiring a compromise of the individual's best judgment. Among the many inhibiting external forces are the following: availability of *personnel, funds, equipment, time, instructional materials,* and *space.* All are complicated by existing *administrative rules and policies.* Any one of these conditions can produce devastating effects on the best of intentions. Each must be considered in relation to the particular situation.

SELECTION GUIDELINES

When writing about T/L techniques, authors universally refrain from stating hard and fast rules for teachers to follow in the selection process. Most authors, however, do provide general guidelines based upon conventional wisdom, experience, and/or research. Among the more helpful suggestions are the following:

1. *Match activities with the behavior specified in the objective.*

This principle is based on the assumption that different objectives require different developments and applications. The teacher's role is to provide students with practice in performing the action described in the objective. The action may be a physical skill, a cognitive skill, a social skill, or an affective skill. By making a careful analysis, the performance is identified and a matching T/L technique is selected.

a. Developing Skills

Developing skills involves acquiring greater expertness of performance. In this chapter the term is broadly defined to include the psychomotor skills common to industrial education, music, art, and physical education programs; the social skills of leadership, cooperation, and group participation; and the cognitive skills of analysis, evaluation, and synthesis.

Skill development lessons usually require two conditions: (1) an explanation or a description of the skill and (2) practice of the skill. Neither explanation nor practice is adequate by itself to produce the desired result. Both are necessary to assure the development of skills.

Excessive practice of any skill may lead to fatigue and possibly to a decrease in the level of performance. If the exercise is too difficult, frustration and premature fatigue may occur. Spacing practice at intervals is therefore advisable.

Because social activity involves personal interactions, the interaction techniques are most effective for developing social skills.

b. Developing Feelings

Attitudes are more easily revised by positive activities. Affective objectives usually require setting up a situation or a characterization toward which students can react emotionally. Such techniques as discussions and role-playing give students an opportunity to test and experience the behaviors stated in these objectives.

2. *Provide variety.*

Even the most dedicated racing fans would tire of watching "the greatest spectacle in racing," the Indianapolis 500, every day. Our senses soon tire of a uniform stimulus. The human mind needs a change of pace or it becomes bored. With the skillful use of varied and interesting T/L techniques, the probability of boredom setting in can be significantly reduced.

3. *Plan active student involvement* (mental, physical, and personal).

Student activity is an integral part of action and interaction techniques. The student may be passive when presentation techniques are used, however, unless provisions are made for some sort of involvement. The following suggestions should encourage students to become more active during presentations and should reduce the tendency to be uninvolved.

- Keep presentations short.
- Provide response forms to complete during the presentation.
- Ask students to contribute information whenever possible.
- Let students help in the presentation by holding objects or performing tasks.
- Let students assist in the demonstration of a skill.

4. *Provide feedback.*

The kind, extent, and validity of feedback affect present and subsequent learning. Valid feedback provides meaning and new direction to learning. Evaluation of progress in reaching a goal enhances learning.

5. *Provide positive models.*

Modeling is learning by observing others perform correctly. It is especially preferred in teaching physical skills; and it is growing in popularity in developing interpersonal communication skills. Students achieve competencies more quickly if models of desired behaviors (a skill or a product of student efforts) are supplied early in the instructional process. Modeling requires that the student (1) *observe* the correct behavior being performed, (2) *practice* the behavior, and (3) receive intrinsic and/or extrinsic *rewards* for performing the behavior correctly.

6. *Plan activities that are appropriate to student readiness and needs.*

Students should have the educational, physical, intellectual, and emotional development necessary to participate in learning activities. Most important of all, they should be interested in them. An intent to learn is essential for purposeful learning. Attempt to match each activity to a basic student need—the need to be successful, to be recognized, to be accepted, to be respected, or to be active.

7. *Provide challenge.*

The ability to accept challenge varies greatly between individuals and from one time to another within the individual. A student may accept high risks in athletic activities but may prefer low-risk cognitive activities. Whatever the preference, activities should be designed so that they are challenging enough to arouse student interest, yet not so challenging that they discourage it. Knowledge of the student's level of confidence in each area of interest is necessary if this guideline is to be applied effectively.

8. *Match activities with learning styles.*

Those who read well should be given the opportunity to use that mode, just as the "listeners" and "doers" should be provided the opportunity to capitalize on their strengths. Attempts to help students build skill in using learning styles that they have not yet fully developed should not be entirely rejected. Students who are unable to learn effectively by any one of the modalities are somewhat handicapped, and attempts should be made to correct these handicaps.

9. *Involve students in realia.*

Let students observe, handle, inspect, and otherwise experience actual objects. Let them assist in demonstrations, using models and actual objects while demonstrations are being conducted.

10. *Provide activities with several levels of accomplishment.*

An activity which accommodates a wide variety of abilities at different levels will make success possible for a larger number of students than one with rigid standards.

Figure 4 is presented only as a summary of these selection guidelines and as a means of contrasting, in a visual format, the limited potential of some popular T/L techniques and the flexibility of others. It should not be interpreted as the final word on the use of these techniques to achieve a particular objective.

Figure 4.
TEACHING/LEARNING TECHNIQUE SELECTION GUIDE

T/L TECHNIQUES*			Affective					Psychomotor					Cognitive					
			Characterizing	Organizing	Valuing	Responding	Receiving	Perfecting	Performing	Manipulating	Imitating	Perceiving	Evaluation	Synthesis	Analysis	Application	Comprehension	Knowledge
Presentations	Lectures	Formal					●										●	●
		Informal					●										●	●
		Guest					●										●	●
	Demonstrations	Manipulative					●					●						●
		Principle					●					●						●
		Device					●					●						●
	A/V	Presentation					●					●					●	●
		Model					●				●	●						●
	Field Trips						●					●					●	●
Actions	Projects	Producer				●		●	●	●	●		●	●	●	●	●	
		Problem-Solving			●	●		●	●	●	●		●	●	●	●	●	
		Specific Skill				●			●	●	●					●	●	
	Experiments					●	●				●	●				●	●	●
	Exercises					●	●				●	●				●	●	●
	Guided Observations						●					●				●	●	●
Interactions	Questioning				●	●	●						●	●	●	●	●	●
	Discussions				●	●	●						●	●	●	●	●	●
	Buzz Sessions			●	●	●	●										●	●
	Brainstorming					●	●										●	●
	Seminars					●	●					●					●	●
	Interviewing					●	●					●					●	●
	Role-Playing					●	●				●	●				●	●	●
	Gaming					●	●											●
	Committees					●	●										●	●
	Debates	Observing					●											●
		Participating				●	●								●	●	●	●

*An explanation of the potential use of these T/L techniques included in chapters 6, 7, and 8 describes their planning, implementation, and evaluation.

Chapter 6.

PLANNING PRESENTATION TECHNIQUES
(Using Presentation Tools)

Purpose: As saws are to furniture builders, so presentations are to teachers. Every part of a piece of furniture must first be cut to size with a saw before any other operations are performed. Similarly, presentations are used to introduce, to provide background information, and to direct student activities before application activities are started.

Objective: After selecting a presentation technique, you will be able to plan the technique well enough so that a knowledgeable person can implement the lesson using your lesson plan.

Presentation techniques have dominated the teaching scheme for hundreds of years. Many believe that they are overused in the classroom and over emphasized in teacher preparation programs. When simple guidelines are followed, however, presentation techniques are efficient in presenting management and subject matter information in a consistent, organized manner.

The specific techniques included in this chapter are formal, informal, and guest lectures; demonstrations of manipulative skills, physical principles, and mechanical devices; audiovisual presentations; and field trips. Explanations of each technique will cover the following points:

1. Brief description
2. Recommended application
3. Planning procedure
4. Implementation recommendations
5. Evaluation

LECTURES

Lectures are exciting learning techniques if they are well planned and skillfully delivered. To be effective, the lecturer must commit sufficient time to organize and adapt the topic to the audience and to rehearse and polish the delivery. Since this kind of preparation requires a great deal of time, the number of skillfully done formal lectures may be small. Most teachers prefer the informal lecture in which students participate and which therefore has the advantage of being more interesting to students.

If either of these forms of the lecture is supplemented with visuals and objects, it is called an *illustrated lecture.* When accompanied by a demonstration, it is a *lecture-demonstration.*

1. *Formal Lecture*

A formal lecture is an oral exposition of facts, principles, procedures, feelings, or directions by the teacher. It is a strong, versatile, and efficient way of bringing the lecturer's views immediately into focus. Further, essential factual material not found in the reading can be presented vividly by a skillful lecturer. Effective utilization is the key to the lecture's success, as with all T/L techniques.

In PLANNING the formal lecture, the following guidelines may be of assistance.

Phase I. Planning the Topic

- Choose the topic.
- Explore the topic in your own mind.
- Determine the point of view.
- Differentiate between fact and opinion.
- Research the topic in standard references.
- Develop a perspective on the topic.

Phase II. Planning the Implementation

- Select effective terms and expressions.
- Determine the length.
- Establish the depth.
- Select illustrations and examples.
- Redo the degree of abstraction with visuals, dramatizations, and demonstrations.
- Plan for audience participation (structure note taking or problems to solve).

The following approaches to organizing formal lectures may also be helpful.

a. "Little Method" Format

Although the "Little Method" developed by St. Vincent was designed to teach moral behavior, it has wide application for educators. It is effective for communicating topics which consist of terms, places, methods, or processes that can be described and explained. It is the responsibility of the lecturer to devise the packaging of the concept into a form that students will enjoy.

A simple, direct, and straightforward presentation, the "Little Method" format has three components:

(1) A description of the characteristics of the topic—what is being studied

(2) The motivation for the audience to become involved in learning about the topic—why the topic is being studied

(3) An explanation of the topic—how one can learn about the topic or put the idea into practice.

b. Parable Format

In the parable format the lecturer introduces a new and different concept by comparing it to one that is familiar to the audience. The comparison of the skilled furniture builder and the creative teacher is an example of this application.

The parable is highly flexible. It is effective from kindergarten through adulthood and can be motivating if the new concept is compared to something that is familiar and valued by the learner. This format consists of three parts:

(1) The *statement of the analogy* compares the new concept to the familiar one (creative teaching is like building fine furniture) or points out the relevant and comparable points (material—students and content, specifications—objectives, etc.).

(2) In the core of the lecture, the *details* of the known concept are used to explain and give meaning to the details of the new topic.

(3) As the analogy is closed, conclusions are drawn. When the student understands the analogy, the learning has occurred.

2. Informal Lecture

The informal lecture may be patterned after the formal lecture format. The rigidity of the formal lecture is reduced, however, because there are opportunities for students to interject ideas, to ask questions, and to provide examples from their own experiences during the informal lecture.

Informal lectures may be used to provide background information on a topic or content area, to introduce a major unit, to carry the main load of information for a unit, to summarize a segment of instruction, or to stimulate a person to behave in a particular way. Regardless of the purpose, the objective for this technique should be clearly in mind.

The following generalized format is suggested for the informal lecture:

- *Define terms.* Explain words, expressions, and other new symbols necessary for an understanding of the concepts.
- *Outline details.* Break down the topic into parts and subparts to its simplest and most easily understood elements.
- *Summarize.* Close the lecture by reviewing, condensing, and repeating its principal points.
- *Raise and answer questions.* Allow students an opportunity to ask questions, to clarify misunderstandings, and to put the points of the lecture into perspective with their own life circumstances.

FOR IMPLEMENTATION of the lecture, students should be prepared in advance on the nature and amount of freedom they will have for participation. Student interest will be maintained by the use of stimulus variation which was discussed in the Introduction. Teachers can facilitate student learning and note taking by—

- Using a consistent outline to present material.
- Explaining the organization of the lecture.
- Emphasizing the main ideas.
- Restating and rephrasing complex points.
- Using examples.
- Using contextual clues (e.g., "There are four ways of . . ." to introduce a list of points).
- Including some pauses to allow for note taking.
- Distributing note-taking aids.
- Distributing problems related to the material and asking students to listen for relevant information to solve the problems.

Teachers can instruct their students in methods of note taking by suggesting that they write down only key phrases, use personal shorthand, and keep notes neat so that recopying is unnecessary.

3. *Guest Lecture*

Teachers often have the option of making a presentation themselves or of inviting someone else to make a presentation. A lecture by a guest has several advantages—utilizing expert knowledge or skills, providing variety, and presenting an alternative point of view—all of which can enrich class activities.

Procedures for the guest lecture usually include the following:

- *Orientation.* Introduction of the speaker with a description of the person's position, experience, and special qualifications; the reason the person was asked; the topic to be covered; and the follow-up procedures.
- *Development.* Presentation by the speaker.

- *Follow-Up.* Expressions of thanks to the speaker, questions, discussion, and other follow-up activities.

DEMONSTRATIONS

The demonstration is an example of teaching by showing. This technique employs sight and touch rather than hearing as the major means of communication. Manipulative skills, physical principles, and the working of mechanical devices are often more effectively taught by demonstrations than by other methods.

Although there seems to be no standard format for the demonstration, most authors include similar components under one description or another. These components are sometimes modified to satisfy peculiarities of the concept to be learned or the teaching situation. Most often included are the following elements:

Orientation—includes the purpose, the objective, and/or the tie-in information

Development—with the following subcomponents:

- *Presentation—consists of a preview, a detailed presentation, and a review*
- *Discussion—clarifies misunderstanding and fills gaps*
- *Application—includes reinforcing questions, practice, and/or other imitation activities carried on by one or more students*

Follow-up—an assignment that encourages higher skill development, the transfer of learning, a broader understanding of the concept, and/or a clearer, more detailed comprehension of the concept.

The following procedure will be helpful in PLANNING demonstrations:

- *Identify* the relevant skill, concept, or mechanism.
- *Outline* key points such as procedural steps of a manipulative skill, relevant variables in a physical principle, or the parts and their

relationship to each other in the mechanical device.

● *Rehearse* by testing equipment and working through the demonstration.

As in all T/L techniques, the IMPLEMENTATION of the demonstration is crucial to its success. The following list of guidelines can contribute to this success:

● Have tools, equipment, and visuals available and in good condition.

● Arrange students so that all can see the demonstration.

● Model correct, accurate, and safe work habits.

● Demonstrate one procedure at a time.

● Present only essential information and theory.

● Use visuals for things that are not fully visible.

● ALWAYS have an application activity following the demonstration.

● Time the demonstration so that it is given when students are ready to use the skill, principle, or knowledge.

Because timing is so important and so often ignored, special attention should be given this idea: *Give the demonstration when students are ready.* In principle, this suggestion sounds fine, but in practice it may be necessary to give the demonstration to the group when a few advanced students are ready and then review it later for the slower ones. An alternative would be to divide the group, giving separate demonstrations—first to the faster students and at a later date to the slower ones.

EVALUATION may be accomplished by informal observations to find answers to the following questions:

● Were the purpose, objective, and/or tie-in clear?

● Were all materials ready?

● Could all students see?

● Were safety precautions observed?

● Were students directly involved in the demonstration?

● Was the timing right?

● Did the demonstration work?

● Were sufficient visuals available?

● Could students perform the task, explain the principle, or describe the mechanism after the demonstration was over?

1. *Manipulative Skill Demonstration*

Probably no other technique is more often used than the demonstration in teaching manipulative skills. The technique capitalizes on the visual sense, the sense that receives the greatest amount of information and is the most difficult to turn off or distract.

When preparing for a demonstration of a manipulative skill, carefully analyze the procedure and list each procedural step in order. Identify related information, making certain to include safety precautions, safety margins, and necessary safety equipment. Interweave relevant information, but be aware of the amount of time to be used for the demonstration.

The initial "showing" step can be expected to develop only *knowledge* about a manipulative skill (the perceiving level in the psychomotor domain). Such knowledge should include the following elements:

● Steps

● Purpose for each step

● Relationship of each step in the sequence

● Physical motion necessary to perform the task

● Skilled person performing the skill correctly in a work situation, if possible.

Higher skill levels can be developed only with practice. Well-selected follow-up activities or projects are essential when high-level performance is the goal.

2. *Physical Principle Demonstration*

Physical principles are commonly demonstrated in the sciences. Simple machines, current flow, and the effects of sound and light can all be demonstrated in physics classes, for example. In most courses the understanding of the principle as well as the application are emphasized. Therefore, demonstrations of principles are often accompanied by manipulative activities which apply the principles.

In planning such a demonstration, first carefully analyze the resources describing the principle. They may be used to identify the contributing factors and the roles they play in the principle. In the case of black surfaces absorbing more radiated heat than white surfaces, for instance, the color of the surfaces and the amount of radiant heat are the variables.

Next, design T/L activities which make it possible for the student to experience the variables. To carry forward the example, cut two identical pieces of sheet metal, painting one black and one white. Place them in a sunny window for ten minutes. Then ask a student to feel the pieces of metal and report to the class which feels warmer than the other.

Finally, identify activities in which the principle is applied. For example, students may design simple solar collectors for homes and test their efficiency.

3. *Mechanical Device Demonstration*

Using only written or spoken words to describe the working of anything but the simplest mechanical device is at best difficult. A demonstration that includes the manipulation of the actual object, a cutaway or scaled model, and pictures or drawings of invisible parts is a more successful approach.

In demonstrations of mechanical devices, the aim is to make clear to learners the function of each part and the relationship of the parts to each other. In planning such a demonstration, analyze thoroughly the parts of the mechanism and their relation to each other. Organize the demonstration in the most logical manner.

There are several ways to make the presentation, but the following procedure is quite common:

1) Orientation
   (a) Purpose, tie-in, and/or objective

2) Development
   (a) Presentation
      —Parts
      —Function of parts
      —Relationship of parts
   (b) Application
      —Drill exercise
      —Use of device
3) Follow-up
   (a) Questions
   (b) Explanation by students
   (c) Project requiring use of device

AUDIOVISUAL PRESENTATIONS

Audiovisual (AV) materials are used extensively and effectively in individualized instruction systems. In this book, however, their use will be limited to classroom groups. Filmstrips, recordings, motion pictures, slide series, video programs, or combinations are grouped together here because the procedure for using each format is the same.

Audiovisual presentations consist of a *set* sequence of still or motion pictures, an audio narration, or a combination of both that is presented to the learner. Rather than being the message carrier in this T/L technique, the teacher arranges for the operation or manipulation of the carrier and is primarily responsible for preparing the group for the presentation and for planning the application experiences.

Presentations employing AV materials can bring sights and sounds to the classroom that are otherwise unavailable—sights and sounds that are too small, too large, too expensive, too perishable, too soft, too far away, too fast, too slow, too old, or too rare. Learners can also benefit from how-to lessons which may be presented effectively and consistently through the use of this medium. Finally, materials that show positive performance models of manipulative skills and interpersonal communication skills can assist teaching in these areas. Familiarity with AV materials and the careful planning of their use can increase the quality and diversity of teaching without significantly increasing the work load.

As in all T/L techniques, three phases are involved in making AV presentations:

PLANNING

- *Identify* potential materials through the use of AV catalogs and directories.

- *Select* materials based upon the objectives to be achieved.

- *Prepare* to use the materials. Preview them and read the teacher's guides. Take notes. Enlist students' help in previewing. Students may see things that are not apparent to the teacher.

- *Plan lesson content and procedures* relating them to the purpose for use of the materials, student focus, and the method of presenting the materials.

IMPLEMENTATION

- *Orientate* students by stating reasons for observing the AV material and what should be gained from the presentation. Point out new words or expressions, and provide a response form which will actively involve students during the presentation and assist them in taking notes.

- *Development*: Present the material. Even in this stage learning may be increased by a little creativity. If the content is complex or is presented at a fast pace, a replay may help students. Sometimes only a portion of the material may be suitable. Important points or corrections may be made during the presentation by stopping or restarting the particular item.

- *Application*: Relate the content of the material to the reality of the class topic.

- *Follow-up activities* may reinforce learning by providing opportunities for practice and transfer related to the AV presentation. (If the film shows how to strike an arc and run a bead with an electric arc welder, for example, students may be given exercises to practice the skill. Industrial management activities shown in a film may be transferred to the management of a student-operated corporation.) Here again teacher creativity is important.

EVALUATION may be accomplished by answering the following questions:

- Did the AV presentation fit the objective?

- Did the AV presentation help achieve the objective?

- How did students respond to the AV presentation?

- Were the application activities appropriate?

- Was the presentation suitable to the age group?

FIELD TRIPS

A field trip or tour is a carefully arranged visit by a group to an object or place of interest for firsthand observation and study. It may vary from a short visit to a single location to an excursion lasting several days and covering several states. *Minitrips* are trips taken within the school (a communication class views the school's intercommunication system in the main office). *Miditrips* are those taken within the immediate community (a visit to a construction site across the street from the school). Finally, *maxitrips* are a day or more in length and require transportation (a visit to the historical monuments in Washington, D.C.).

Field trips serve six basic purposes:

1. As *introductory experiences* they serve to develop a broad general understanding of the topic to be studied. (Prior to studying a unit in "Communicating with Electronics," the class is taken to a radio or television studio to see it in operation.)

2. *Summary or review* activities are used as capstone experiences to crystallize and verify a number of related units or concepts that were presented earlier in the course. (When nearing the end of an automobile maintenance course, the class is taken to a large auto distributor's service area to view procedures, practices, and policies used in a commercial establishment.)

3. *Interest is developed* when a highly interesting trip is selected. (One way to develop

interest in the concept of automation is to visit a modern bottling plan or bakery.)

4. *Data collecting* is possible by taking a group of students to a location where they may make observations and record them for use in completing a project. (Science students visit streams to collect water, soil, vegetation, and other biological specimens to study in the classroom.)

5. *Enrichment, variety, or challenge* may be provided with field trips. (Skill in reading compasses and field instruments is tested on an orienterring field trip.)

6. *Broadened cultural experiences* are enjoyed by student visits to museums, art galleries, theaters, concert halls, zoos, and the like. (Both an art class and a social studies class benefit from a visit to a special exhibit such as the King Tut.)

To insure that the maximum benefit is gained from the field trip, the following three functions should be performed carefully:

PLANNING

- *Identify* the variety of possibilities for field trips by reading school bulletins and announcements, newspapers and journals; by asking colleagues for recommendations; and by checking the yellow pages of the telephone book. Then determine if and when appropriate tours are given, the ages and number of students who are accepted, and any other relevant information.

- *Select* the most appropriate trip from these possibilities after considering school policies, objectives to be developed, time allowed, transportation available, and other school-oriented constraints.

- *Prepare* for the field trip by making arrangements for such details as transportation, food, rest periods, school clearance, parental permission, supervision, and safety. Also determine routes, schedules, and dress codes. In addition, preparation includes the development of student preparation and response forms, and follow-up activities.

IMPLEMENTATION

(Note: Because of the possibility of serious liability ramifications, all managerial details relating to behavior, safety, routes, schedules, supervision, and school clearance should be attended to before implementation.)

- *Orientate* students by making clear to them why they are taking the field trip, what the objectives are, and/or how the trip fits into other classroom activities.

- *Develop* the presentation by asking questions which (1) bring observations in line with the objectives, (2) assist in maintaining schedules, and (3) encourage student involvement. In ensuing discussions, help students to apply what they have seen on the trip and to synthesize their experiences into their own frames of reference.

- *Follow up* by asking students to prepare reports or other appropriate materials incorporating their experiences. Provide some questions or suggestions. If specimens or data were collected, have students prepare a bulletin board or report using these items.

EVALUATION

- Can students answer the prepared questions?

- Would other techniques have worked as well as the field trip?

- Were there any unexpected problems relating to the briefing, guides, schedules, trip conditions, or student behavior?

- Did the students' new learning and interest balance out the costs in terms of time, energy, and expenses?

SUMMARY

Presentations are the most commonly used of T/L techniques. They are exciting and useful when properly planned and implemented. By following the preceding suggestions and recommendations, student motivation, interest, and learning may be greatly faciliated.

Chapter 7.

PLANNING ACTION TECHNIQUES
(Using Action Tools)

Purpose: The furniture builder uses different operations and tools to plane, drill, and smooth wood. Similarly, when teachers want to achieve objectives in different domains, different T/L techniques are needed. This chapter introduces the action techniques which provide students with an opportunity to apply and/or practice the behaviors stated in the objectives.

Objective: After selecting the specific action technique to meet your objective, you will be able to prepare a lesson plan that describes the use of the technique so that another knowledgeable person can implement the lesson.

Action techniques directly involve the learner with ideas, materials, objects, and equipment. Individually or in small subgroups, students experiment, construct, observe, and otherwise manipulate things for a variety of purposes.

One of the most familiar uses of action techniques is to provide students with opportunities to *practice a skill, procedure, or process* described in the objective. In this case, the action technique usually follows a presentation that describes or demonstrates the skill and it is used as an application or a follow-up activity. Typing exercises or dribbling a basketball are examples.

Action techniques are also used to *develop and understand a cognitive principle or concept.* A presentation may be followed by an experiment verifying the principle or concept which is intended to increase understanding. To illustrate, the teacher may lecture on the concept of interchangeable parts, followed by an experiment in which two groups assemble the parts of ball point pens. One group has the parts for twenty-five pens that are alike. The other group has the parts for twenty-five pens that are different. Comparing the speed of the two groups in assembling the pens will contribute to an understanding of the concept of interchangeable parts.

Closely related to this use of action techniques are the *observation of phenomena* and the *transfer of a principle, skill, or process to a new situation.* For example, the mechanical advantage of pulleys can be observed by conducting laboratory experiments with apparatus set up in the classroom. These principles can be transferred to everyday situations by asking students to analyze the pulley systems used in hoists in automobile garages to lift heavy parts, or on farms to lift hay into barns and to stretch fences.

Another use of action techniques is to *develop problem-solving skills.* Objectives directly related to this use are often stated for many curriculum areas—industrial arts, science, home economics, and mathematics, for example. Student projects are described as problems rather than objects to be built and lead to action techniques which develop problem-solving skills. An example might be a situation in which students have to sit on metal stools in the industrial arts laboratory. When the stoools are moved, they scrape and ring with an irritating sound. The problem, then, is to reduce the noise level rather than build cushioned feet for the stools.

The kinds of action techniques to be discussed include projects, exercises, experiments, and guided observations. Three kinds of projects, one exercise, one experiment, and one guide observation will be treated in detail with a description and an example for each.

PROJECTS

Projects, defined in a broad sense, include any undertaking by an individual or group that results in a tangible product. The product may be a written paper, a bulletin board, a photo essay, a smooth-running engine, or a sculpture, to name only a few. Projects provide students with opportunities to learn a technique, to practice a skill, to illustrate a principle, to solve a problem, or to perform creatively. They offer excellent opportunities for students to pursue personal interests and goals and to learn long-range planning skills. With this definition as a focus, several different types of projects will be considered in detail.

- *Producer projects.* This kind of project is often selected when the objective is to develop creative expression, to capitalize on student interest, or to get students involved in productive effort. The materials and final product have no bounds.

- *Consumer projects.* These activities require only passive student involvement. Observing workers in a work environment, visiting a retirement home, and attending a crafts display are examples of such vicarious learning experiences.

- *Problem-solving projects.* Activities of this type have as their major thrust the purpose of clearing up some technical or intellectual question or difficulty. They are popular in the sciences, in industrial education, and in mathematics. The project is usually preceded by a presentation and an exercise involving the problem-solving procedure. The solution can be displayed in many ways—writing, speaking, singing, drawing.

- *Specific skill development projects.* Skill in this context involves a range of cognitive and psychomotor abilities varying from the lowest level to the highest level in each domain. Writing skills can be developed by having students complete term paper projects; stitchery skills can be achieved by having students complete pillow covers or similar projects.

All types of projects have usefulness to the educator. In the consumer project, however, the student is a passive observer. Since there is no direct involvement in physical activity with materials or equipment, this is not an action technique and it will not be treated here. Procedures for implementing such activities are quite similar, and in some cases identical, to those used for field trips which are discussed in Chapter 6.

A successful project activity involves teacher/student cooperation to identify an area of meaningful interest. If the project has no definite or meaningful purpose, there is a distortion of the technique which leads to a mere performance of a task. Use of the technique should include the following functions:

- *Orientation.* Students must understand, feel, and identify with the reasons for the project.

- *Planning.* Thorough planning is essential. In preparation, the student uses a variety of resources and develops a variety of researching skills. From this investigation, an outline or plan is made and agreed upon.

- *Implementation.* In this phase, the plan is put into action. The better the plan, the more direct and efficient the student activity.

- *Evaluation.* At this time student and teacher judge the results of the project. Most importantly, they assess what the learner gained from the project. What new terms, knowledge, skills, and feelings were learned? How well were they learned?

In evaluating the success of the project as a T/L technique, the teacher needs to be cognizant of such considerations as the following:

- Was the emphasis placed on the learning or on competition for the largest, most expensive project?

- Were qualities of originality, cooperation, persistence, and responsibility rewarded?

- Was the major focus student growth or the quality of the project?

- Did the student understand the purpose of the project?

- Was the planning satisfactory?

● Was the execution of the project possible and efficient?

1. *Producer Project*

The producer project is the most flexible of all projects. It is very useful when the objective of the lesson is broad and permits a wide range of expression to demonstrate growth and when numerous ways exist to develop relevant knowledge and experience. When studying the concept of mass transportation in 2000 A.D., for example, several students may choose to make a bulletin board that communicates one dimension of the problem. Another student may design and build a model of a vehicle to be used in the futuristic transportation system. Although the two projects are diverse, both contribute to the understanding of the concept. All that is necessary for the success of this T/L technique is that the student choose a project related to the unit objective, that the student identify with the project, and that the project be feasible.

When PLANNING producer projects:

● Be flexible.

● Help students identify and plan their projects.

● Be prepared to provide individual guidance when necessary.

● Have a variety of how-to materials available.

● Give many individual presentations.

● Help students solve a wide variety of problems.

To IMPLEMENT this technique, *orientate* students by—

● Communicating the importance of the concept (individual transportation vehicles are congesting our city streets, polluting our air, and using up our resources).

● Relating the instructional aim or objective to the project (to develop greater understanding in selected areas of the transportation dilemma by completing the project).

In fact, if two students watch and interact with each other as they work on separate undertakings, both students will be involved in a consumer project. As noted earlier, one can learn by watching another engage in an activity.

To *develop* the lesson, background information on the topic or concept is presented. In the presentation, the scope of the topic is described. In the example of the transportation dilemma, students are introduced to the magnitude of the problem of transporting people and other resources in and out of cities. That situation may then be contrasted with the problems of congesting the streets, depleting the resources, and polluting the air. The specifics may be verified by analyzing the circumstances of the student's own city or a nearby city. The application portion should provide such management information as timetables and requirements.

The producer project is most often used as a *follow-up* activity. Among the numerous possibilities, the student may prepare a mobile, a display, or a slide series to summarize the concept; design and build a model; write a paper; or make a report to the class.

The EVALUATION of the producer project is essentially the same as that of other projects discussed earlier in this chapter.

2. *Problem-Solving Project*

The problem-solving project is similar to the producer project inasmuch as problems needing solutions will arise whenver the latter technique is employed. The problem-solving project, however, is specifically designed to provide the student with an activity in which one or more of the problem-solving approaches are learned and used.

In PLANNING the problem-solving project, *prepare yourself* by becoming aware of and proficient in the use of a variety of approaches. Then develop presentations to describe the approaches and examples to illustrate them. One difficulty in preparing to use this kind of activity is that of identifying and describing problems without implying solutions. If the teacher implies the solution, the activity is no longer a problem-solving project.

To IMPLEMENT the problem-solving technique, *orientate* students by providing them with a purpose for the skill or learning that results from the activity. There may be a tie-in to past or future uses. In any case, it is essential to make the aim(s) clear to students if the greatest benefit is to be gained from the project.

When *developing* the lesson, present the problem-solving approach(es) students are to employ, in addition to the dimensions of the problem. The background knowledge and skills, which may take several days to develop, include identifying the problem and alternatives, considering alternatives, deciding on the solution, and implementing the solution. In these background sessions, awareness of fundamental concepts and application activities will assist in developing an adequate level of performance.

This type of project may be a one-day undertaking designed as an application activity to develop more knowledge about a problem-solving approach (selecting a mode of transportation for a trip); or it may be a longer range activity designed to develop high-level skills in seeking solutions to complex problems (designing a mass transit system for a city).

Follow-up activities may include evaluation (as discussed earlier), student presentations to the class, or exhibiting the project to persons outside the classroom or school.

3. *Specific Skill Development Project*

The specific skill development or learning project is used to provide students with an opportunity to practice specific cognitive and psycho-motor skills. It is probably one of the best understood techniques used in industrial and vocational education, music, art, and home economics programs that emphasize skill development. One of the difficulties of its use is the selection of the project. The task is much easier if the performance levels in the psychomotor domain are understood.

For this technique teachers usually demonstrate the skills needed and then have students *imitate* the skill. The next level, *manipulation*, is achieved by letting students apply the skill to an activity similar to the project to be undertaken. At higher levels of performance, students apply the operation to diverse projects and finally vary the operation procedures in acceptable ways or develop new procedures. The specific learning project is more adaptable to lower levels of performance.

To meet higher performance levels, the problem-solving project or the producer project is more suitable.

PLAN the specific skill development project to encompass the skill(s) that have been identified for student mastery. Examples of this T/L technique include machined metal projects that are designed to include specific operations and specified tolerances for a vocational education class, and making slides of onion root tips for a biology class. Students may be given the opportunity to design their own projects, however, if they include previously identified or agreed-upon operations.

To IMPLEMENT this type of project, *orientate* the student by describing the purpose and/or objective. *Present* the description of a teacher-designed activity, or work cooperatively with the student to design one. Make certain that teacher and student agree upon the project specifications and deadlines. Then, it is important to assist the student, when necessary, to meet these requirements.

EVALUATION is a matter of comparing the project with the agreed-upon specifications. Specifications that are not met should be carefully reviewed to discern the particular problem.

EXPERIMENTS

Experiments are conducted for at least three purposes: (1) to introduce students to the experimental approach to collecting data; (2) to collect data so that commonalities may be discovered, principles identified, or conclusions drawn; and (3) to verify principles or conclusions.

Two important guidelines to keep in mind when selecting experiments are to make certain that the principle or data is worth verifying or collecting and that students are interested in the topic.

In PLANNING the experiment:

- Clarify the problem.
- Specifically identify the data to be collected and what is to be done with it.
- Organize the procedures.
- Prepare the test equipment and supplies.
- Use simple (but not crude) apparatus.

- Test the apparatus.
- Prepare any needed guide sheets.
- Decide on the student grouping method.
- Identify and specify safety precautions.

When IMPLEMENTING the experiment, *orientate* students by describing its purpose, how it ties into other activities, and the specific objectives to be accomplished.

In the presentation portion of the *development,* describe the experimental procedures, distribute guide sheets, caution students about safety, establish groups, and state time limits. In the application portion, students conduct the experiment, collect and summarize data.

In the *follow-up* section of the lesson, students report findings, draw conclusions, and apply the conclusions.

EVALUATION is accomplished by referring to the planning criteria to determine if they were met. If the criteria were not met, corrections should be made so that the technique will be more effective when used again.

EXERCISES

Unlike projects, exercises involve the completion of a task rather than a tangible product. Exercises are especially adapted to the practice and/or use of complex psychomotor and cognitive skills. These complex behaviors are actually a composite of several individual tasks. For example, developing a roll of film involves the ability to use a darkroom timer, to open a film cassette, to remove the exposed film, to load the film on the developing tank reel, to adjust the temperature of the chemicals, and to perform several other individual tasks. In teaching such a procedure, it is well to provide opportunities for the student to rehearse handling film cassettes and loading reels in the light with a practice film before attempting the entire task with exposed film in a darkroom or changing bag.

When using this technique, it is recommended that necessary equipment, partially prepared materials, and printed procedures be provided so that students may work through the exercise with ease.

The PLANNING, IMPLEMENTATION, and EVALUATION of exercises are similar to those used in demonstrations of manipulative skills. Detailed directions are provided in Chapter 6.

GUIDED OBSERVATIONS

Guided observations are most often used when topics are introduced. This activity is effective in helping students become aware of the particular characteristics of an object, the parts of a device, or other critical variations. For example, to teach map reading, the topic may be introduced by explaining the different kinds of maps and their general characteristics and purposes. Numbered examples of each map may then be distributed and students asked to name the maps verbally, to write the names in numbered blanks, or to match the names with numbers on a response form. Individual creativity will provide numerous other ways of using guided observations to help students become aware of the important variations involved in concepts.

To PLAN a guided observation:

- Become familiar with the topic.
- Identify the specific characteristics of which students should become aware.
- Collect a comprehensive set of examples that include one or more illustrations of each characteristic to be identified.
- Plan the observation procedure.
- Design the response form.
- Reproduce the response form, if necessary.
- Decide how to provide feedback to students.

To IMPLEMENT the technique, simply *orientate* students to the topic and to its value.

Develop the topic by presenting subject matter information on its scope and the important characteristics of which students need to become aware. Management information describing the procedure to be used by students in observing phenomena, in making their responses, and in reporting their responses is also included in the presentation.

In the *follow-up,* student responses are reported and discussed. The discussion provides the feedback that helps to crystallize the learning. Finally, a summary at the end of the session may facilitate closure for students.

To EVALUATE the guided observations, observe the following:

- Adherence of students to procedures
- Accuracy of student observations
- Relevancy of examples to the characteristics
- Adequacy of time allotted for the activity
- Willingness and enthusiasm of student participation.

SUMMARY

Students like to do things that interest them, and they learn from such activities. Performance objectives lead toward action techniques. This is especially true when student achievement at the higher levels in the domains of learning is the target of the instruction. When preparing objectives, think "higher levels" and "student activity." Knowledge and identification of student interests will lead to action techniques which will become more interesting and challenging to both students and teacher alike.

Chapter 8.

PLANNING INTERACTION TECHNIQUES
(Using Interaction Tools)

Purpose: When furniture makers find a set of tools that make it possible to convert once-wasted materials into profitable and attractive pieces, they obtain the tools and learn to use them. Teachers have a set of tools that, with skillful use, can convert excessive idle chatter into exciting and informative exchanges of ideas. These exchanges, or interaction techniques, often result in positive growth in student understandings, skills, and attitudes. Ten of these T/L tools are discussed in this chapter.

Objective: After selecting the specific interaction technique to meet your objective, you will be able to prepare a lesson plan that describes the use of the technique so that another knowledgeable person can implement the lesson.

Exchanging ideas through talking is as natural to young people as drinking soda. When the bell rings to end a class period, the rate of speaking increases sharply to a high pitch. In the hallways, the exchange of ideas may be referred to as pandemonium, a madhouse, or some other, perhaps more descriptive, term.

Interaction techniques are designed to capitalize on the human desire to talk and share ideas. Personal interaction is an activity in which two or more people are actively involved in exchanging ideas. Therein lies one major advantage of these techniques: Students become valued resources, vital and necessary elements of the T/L environment. Their ideas and efforts are received and respected.

In this environment, the teacher plays an important role. It is the teacher who creates groups of the appropriate size and with the necessary skills, and who helps the groups identify attractive and attainable goals. To achieve these ends, the teacher must be proficient in soliciting, understanding, and reacting to each student's responses.

Interaction techniques are especially useful when the day's activity centers around—

- Solving a problem in which a number of diverse opinions will contribute to a solution (identifying a way to raise funds for a class field trip).

- Responding to a problem that most students will confront when they enter life roles (reacting to unearned criticism).

- Making value judgments (driving within the established speed limit).

- Developing an understanding of and feeling for another point of view (seeing both labor and management views on wages vs. productivity questions).

- Helping members of the class share with each other the results of their efforts and seek assistance in solving individual problems (conducting a weekly or biweekly seminar for students working on producer projects).

- Soliciting information from a specialist in the field related to the unit of study (interviewing a student's parent who is a doctor concerning certain health questions).

In PLANNING interaction techniques the three lesson components are, again, applicable. The *orientation* introduces the learner to the lesson. In the presentation part of the *development,* learners are made aware of the background information and procedures needed to participate in the interaction; and in the application, the activity is actually implemented. Each interaction technique becomes more effective when *follow-up* activities are provided—including summaries, evaluations, or assignments.

Interaction techniques to be considered in the following pages include questioning, discussions, buzz sessions, brainstorming, seminars, interviewing, role-playing, gaming, committees, and debates.

QUESTIONING

Throughout life people use questions to gain information. In teaching, questions are used extensively in another way—to facilitate learning. The first use of questions to facilitate learning is to *diagnose* student levels of achievement at the beginning of a segment of instruction. When utilized for this purpose, questions are designed to establish the experiential background and interest of students.

The second use is to *assess achievement* at the end of a segment of instruction. Such questions are intended to evaluate each student's understanding of facts and principles and the ability to apply them.

Care should be taken in selecting the questions for summaries and reviews. The type of question may cue students to listen and learn the things asked for. If facts are called for, they will attend to and learn facts. If principles and applications of principles are asked for, then they will concentrate on that kind of learning. Similar behavior may occur in the case of test items.

The third use of questions to facilitate learning is to include them in the orientation of the lesson to *promote interest and motivation.*

When a class is routinely begun by directly stating why the objective is important, how it will be achieved, and how it relates to other lessons, students may become bored rather than motivated. Asking such questions as "What things are necessary to conduct a good experiment?" may provide variety and interest not offered by deductive statements.

The fourth use of questions to facilitate learning is to select queries that encourage students to *think more deeply* on topics and challenge their reasoning power.

The following four types of questions are recommended.

- *Closed questions* fall short of encouraging or developing participation in classroom discussion. They may be either an identification question (What kind of bird is this?), a selection question (Who was right, the plaintiff or the defendant?), or a yes/no question (Is the first step to problem solving to get facts?).

- *Probing questions* are designed to clarify (What do you mean . . .) to justify (Why?), to refocus (to redirect "left field" answers), to expand (Are there other thoughts on this point?), and to reduce (Do you agree?).

- *Divergent or open-ended questions* require the student to think into the future (What will happen or what will it be like when . . .?), to fantasize (What would you do if you were marooned . . .?), or to guess (What would happen if Congress . . .?).

- *Evaluation questions* require the student to make judgments about facts (What is your opinion of . . .?).

When PLANNING to use this technique, prepare the key questions around the major points of the lesson in advance, keeping in mind the following general guidelines:

- Make questions clear and concise by using words that are accurate, familiar, and related to the students' background.

- Include questions that (a) require thought and extended answers (use the words *what, why, how, summarize*); (b) carry the lesson forward (leading questions); and (c) vary in their difficulty.

These qualities of good questions will assist in reaching a greater number of students because variations will be provided that may better match student learning styles and interests. Avoid questions that—

- Suggest their own answers (Who is buried in Grant's tomb?).

- Suggest a "right" answer (Why is walnut a better wood than mahogany?).
- Require students to guess the one right answer from numerous possibilities (What kind of wood is walnut?).
- Are double questions (What is a carburetor and what does it do?).
- Are ambiguous (How does a car work?).

When IMPLEMENTING this technique, consider the following suggestions:

- Ask the question clearly and concisely.
- Provide time for students to formulate answers.
- Call on students by name.
- Ask students to summarize partial answers to questions.
- Involve as many students as possible.
- Reinforce good answers to questions.
- Maintain a balance between calling on volunteers and nonvolunteers.
- Listen to all answers.
- Expect students to evaluate other students' answers.

Bright students can be a problem when using this technique. Often they can and do answer all questions. This willingness to answer is rewarding to the student, but if not controlled, it can alienate the rest of the class. The following recommendations can help keep the entire class involved:

- Let the bright student know you are aware he/she wants to respond and then call on someone else. This will reward the student but prevent one member of the class from dominating the group.
- Use the probing technique called "looping questions" which are designed to fill in information gaps that a brighter student jumped when giving a very perceptive answer.

EVALUATION of the questioning technique is straight-forward. During implementation, discern when questions are stimulating, interesting, and productive, and if student responses are positive. When the symptoms are negative, identify the cause. Look first at the question; analyze each one asked. Are they high-quality questions that avoided the typical mistakes? Do they seem to meet the quality standards stated earlier? If not, change them. If so, try to analyze your question-asking techniques. Were the guidelines followed? The more objective you are, the more successful you will be in identifying and improving your use of this instructional method.

DISCUSSIONS

Discussions are supervised conversations in which informed students take an active role by sharing their ideas about the topic under review. This technique can contribute greatly to individual development. First of all, it is effective in expanding the cognitive and affective dimensions of students. When they prepare themselves on a topic in a variety of ways and then come together to discuss each person's point of view, students will increase their understanding of the topic. Secondly, when a group of people hold differing attitudes that may vary in clarity, a discussion which aims at clarifying values can contribute greatly to developing maturity in the participants.

Thirdly, discussions are beneficial in determining the level of achievement and the attitudes held by students in a particular area.

Finally, this technique has potential for helping students acquire skill in participating in a free exchange of ideas as contributing group members. It affords them the opportunity to express ideas, to share in a verbal interaction, and to work out a logical presentation of points on a topic.

The discussion technique is most useful when the objectives are related to clarifying ideas and values and to problem solving. When well implemented, the technique can result in social growth as well as in individual learning.

In PLANNING for discussions, be certain that—

- The student has sufficient preparation or environmental background to be an efficient participant.

- The classroom atmosphere is sufficiently open to permit effective discussion to occur.

- The seating is flexible (circular seating is recommended).

- The topic is significant to the learner and is sufficiently broad to permit a variety of viewpoints.

The three-component lesson format described earlier is applicable to this technique. It is reaffirmed, however, that variations in this format are possible and are encouraged.

To IMPLEMENT the discussion, participants must have background knowledge about the topic or its related values in order to contribute to the activity. The teacher's role is to guide the group to discern the unifying principle and to provide a democratic classroom atmosphere. A strict, formal, and autocratic atmosphere is incompatible with this activity.

When using the questioning technique described earlier, the teacher is the leader. Discussions, however, may or may not be directed by a leader, although some direction from a leader may be used to guide the group thinking.

The discussion lesson may be organized in the following manner. In the *orientation* a thought-provoking question should be asked. In an environmental science class, for example, the question might be, "What considerations should be kept in mind in developing a policy for protecting an endangered species like the koala bear?"

In the presentation section of the *development,* provide students with an introduction to the problem or topic and solicit their opinions, evaluations, and suggestions. Assure them that their ideas and opinions are valued and respected, even when an idea is not popular. Communicate to students the idea that a discussion is a way of seeking truth, not a place to force individual ideas on others.

In the application section, provide purposeful direction to students throughout the discussion. This is an opportunity to glean each student's points from the interaction and to clarify and unite the ideas in the direction of the lesson's objective. Above all, avoid working toward one *right* answer. Every effort should be made to provide equal opportunity for each participant to contribute so that no one individual dominates the group.

The *follow-up* consists of a review of important points revealed in the discussion. The summary or conclusions can be stated by a student or the teacher.

To EVALUATE the discussion, assess the degree to which—

- Knowledge and attitudes were shared.

- Students listened to and respected each other.

- There was equal participation.

- Opinions were modified.

- Issues were settled or problems solved.

BUZZ SESSIONS

In buzz sessions, the class is divided into small discussion groups of from five to seven students for the purpose of improving student involvement. There are essentially two kinds of buzz sessions. The first is a "planning" buzz session which provides an opportunity for more students to participate in the planning of a future class activity. The objective of the session may be to formulate questions for an interview with a guest or to discover new areas of special interest to be considered as topics for future lessons. When the technique is used in this way, students become involved in the planning without speaking in front of the entire group.

The second kind of buzz session is a "reaction" activity following a major presentation. Members of the subgroup discuss the problems, difficult questions, or controversial issues presented earlier.

Although the purposes of the two kinds of buzz sessions differ greatly, the PLANNING is similar. In both cases:

- Provide flexible seating to facilitate arranging chairs in a circular pattern.,

- Identify leaders and brief them on their duties (leaders are expected to get the discussion going and to insure participation from all members).

- Identify recorders and brief them on their duties (recorders make notes of contributions, summarize them, and present the summary to the entire class).

- Pay attention to the timing of the activities in order to allow time for group reports.

To IMPLEMENT a planning buzz session, *orientate* the group by stating the objectives and reasons for the session. Provide all available relevant information about scheduling and the management of the session in the briefing portion of the *development*. Guard against giving information that might restrict thinking. In the application portion, identify the groups and ask them to begin their discussions. Following the discussions, the groups make their reports.

In the *follow-up* of the planning buzz session, students and/or teacher prepare(s) the final plans for implementing the future lesson.

If the buzz session is designed for the purpose of providing an opportunity for more students to react to a presentation, PLANNING is twofold. First make plans for the presentation and then for the buzz session itself. The only real difference in the planning at this point is that the members of the subgroups will react to questions, problems, or controversial issues found in the presentation. Thereafter, the operation of the reaction buzz session is similar to that of the planning buzz session.

EVALUATION is a matter of determining if the objectives for the session and the topic were achieved. Ask yourself or the participants:

- Did everyone who wished have an opportunity to participate in the session?
- Were fresh ideas for future class topics identified?
- Did perceptive interpretations, points of view, or solutions come from the session?
- Were the timing and other logistics handled well?

BRAINSTORMING

When the quantity of ideas is more desirable than their quality, the brainstorming technique may be used. Brainstorming is a problem-solving activity aimed at stimulating and generating ideas and facilitating their expression. It is most useful in finding solutions to problems that have few easy or obvious solutions.

Group members are asked to suggest as many ideas as possible without the threat of censure or evaluation. Uninhibited and "free-wheeling" solutions are urged with little thought given their practicality.

Successful brainstorming sessions are dependent upon skillful PLANNING. The following recommendations may be helpful:

- Select topics that will elicit responses (How can we transport goods and personnel into our cities more efficiently?).
- Form groups that eliminate unnecessary interference with one another and are of an effective size (from five to eighteen members).
- Assure that the method of recording responses is adequate to record all individual responses (tape recorder or one or more secretaries).
- Instruct group leader(s) to provide passive leadership, to keep the group on the subject, to stop criticism of responses, and to enforce rules for the session.

To IMPLEMENT the technique, the following procedures and content are suggested. *Orientate* students with a statement of anticipated outcomes. In the *development* portion, provide general rules for use of the technique such as the following:

- Make only positive statements.
- Refrain from making judgments or evaluations.
- Encourage imagination.
- Encourage additions to ideas.

Include in the intial presentation the statement of the problem, after which allow thirty seconds of thinking time for participants to organize their thoughts. Then initiate the responding period. During the session, all responses should be recorded by hand or electronically. Terminate the session when the enthusiasm of the groups decreases, giving a one-minute warning before hand.

In the application, ideas are synthesized by the leader, secretary, and/or members of the group. They are then discussed by the group in an effort to combine, evaluate, and/or select material for the follow-up activities.

Results of the brainstorming session are put into action in the *follow-up* activities. Students may use the suggestions gained from the session as possible projects in the form of written reports, models, visuals, working prototypes, drawings of solutions, and other tangible products.

The brainstorming technique is EVALUATED by considering the number of ideas generated, the number of students who participated, and the number of negative responses made, as well as by assessing the variety of ideas and the general attitude of the students involved.

SEMINARS

This technique was developed to facilitate communication and to coordinate the abilities of several individuals. A structured group, the seminar meets periodically or as the group deems necessary. As a community effort, it can contribute to the goals of the group or of individuals by—

- Utilizing each individual's abilities to contribute to the efforts of others.

- Mutually reinforcing each participant's efforts.

- Making the group more cohesive.

- Allowing students to develop skill in communicating at organized meetings.

- Developing proficiency in critically analyzing, challenging, and questioning the ideas and procedures of others.

The seminar chairperson (either teacher or student) is responsible for the PLANNING which includes:

- Preparing the agenda (and reproducing it, if possible)

- Controlling the operation of the seminar

- Introducing guests, presenters, and items on the agenda

- Presiding over all·discussions

- Making sure that items are kept within the time schedule so that all are included.

Tape recorders, progress report cards, and name cards contribute to the efficiency of the seminar.

When IMPLEMENTING a seminar, the main *orientation* usually occurs several days in advance. Students need to know the purpose of the seminar and the benefits to be gained from the activity. The effectiveness of this T/L technique as a means of solving problems and of learning from the experiences of others should be explained. On the day of the seminar, students may be reminded of these benefits.

Conducting the seminar is the *development* portion of the lesson. It is best to follow an agenda which may include such items as the following:

1. Introductions
   —Guests
   —Presentations

2. Progress reports

3. Presentations

4. Discussion and/or questions

5. Individual problems

6. Closing comments
   —Visitors
   —Instructor's summation
   —Chairperson's formal conclusions

The *follow-up* portion may include a summary of presentations, reports, and/or discussions. Students who will be leading future seminars should be reminded of their schedules.

A specific EVALUATION of the seminar may be made by comparing the objective(s) with the results. An informal observation by the teacher or a discussion of the success of the seminar with students is useful. A more general evaluation of the procedures may be made by answering the following questions:

- Were students prepared?

- Was the agenda significant?

- Were guests adequately briefed?

- Did guests make useful contributions?

- Were progress reports organized and clear?

- Were presentations well prepared, well presented, accurate, and complete?

- Were discussions perceptive, well conducted, and relevant?

INTERVIEWING

Interviewing is one of the communicative arts used extensively in journalism and the broadcasting industry. Students who learn to communicate through this process enjoy many opportunities for growth.

There are essentially two approaches for interviewing specialists: the interviewer(s) may go to the specialist or the specialist may come to the school. If only one person is in need of information, the student visits the specialist. Conversely, if the entire group needs information, the specialist is best invited to the school. The final decision and arrangements are governed by the local condition surrounding the situation.

Probably the three most useful characteristics of the interview technique are its inherent mobility, its utilization of community talent, and its availability to the learner seeking potential resources outside the school.

The depth and quality of the information gathered by the interviewer(s) are directly related to the quality of the questions asked, the knowledge of the person being interviewed, and the curiosity and motivation of the interviewer.

Interviewing is both a process and content. As a process, it is an effective method for learning, if well used. In order that the interview be successful, the student must learn several essential skills which become part of the course content. Among these skills are the following:

- Selecting productive talent to interview
- Preparing appropriate questions
- Using a questioning strategy
- Recording and reporting results.

It is evident, then, that the PLANNING for this technique requires more than desk work for the teacher—it requires training sessions for the interviewer.

In these sessions, students need to learn how questions vary both in kind and in quality; how to prepare clear and concise questions that are relevant to the objective of the interview; and how to obtain factual information or extended answers when necessary. (For more information on preparing questions, refer to the earlier discussion in this chapter.) Students will be able to gain more information if they employ a strategy in organizing their questions so that the interview moves forward.

Through these training sessions, students may learn to use a variety of recording methods as well as duplicated question sheets with spaces for responses to help collect and store information and to prepare reports on the interview.

Once they learn how to identify or find out about people with special talents through primary and secondary contacts, students are no longer limited to interviewing friends or neighbors. Other sources of potential talent may be found through faculty recommendations, the yellow pages, and other sources.

Another phase of planning involves teaching students to use the telephone, to write letters of appreciation, and to perform other tasks needed in setting up and carrying out the interview. Thus it is apparent that a good deal of preparation is required before the interview itself.

Several presentation and action techniques are useful in helping students acquire the knowledge portion of the skills just decribed. The skill of interacting productively and confidently, however, is not taught effectively by presentation techniques. By video or audiotaping role-playing sessions of a sample interview and replaying them, students may be provided with complete and accurate feedback on their performances.

When interviewing a visiting specialist at the school, the teacher or students (individually or as a committee) may be responsible for the activities. Much of the detailed planning is the same as that for the guest lecture technique described in Chapter 6.

IMPLEMENTING the interview technique is rather simple if the learner visits the specialist. A more formal approach is needed when the specialist comes to the school.

Orientate the group by stating the purpose(s) of the interview, how it fits into the program, and/or what is to be accomplished.

In the presentation part of the *development*, the interviewee may be introduced by teacher or student as a guest speaker would be introduced. Then the introduction should be followed with an explanation of the floor rules and the line of questioning. Students should be reminded that the guest did not come to debate issues, but to provide information relating to the questions to be asked. (Questions may be sent in advance so that both interviewer and interviewee may be prepared.)

The guest may be asked to make an introductory statement. The interviewing then begins and continues until time runs out or all questions are answered.

Follow-up activities may include a discussion the next day, an application of the new knowledge, or a variety of assignments that utilize the new knowledge.

EVALUATION of both the planning and implementation of the interview is needed. Questions such as the following may be asked:

- Did the questions extract the information sought?

- Did the guest have the necessary background to provide the information sought?

- Were students adequately prepared to ask and respond to questions from the specialist?

- Was the information recorded in a way that made it available to all who needed it?

- Did the interview support or lead to relevant, useful, and interesting follow-up activities?

ROLE-PLAYING

Role-playing may be defined as a method of human interaction that involves realistic, spontaneous behavior in an imaginary situation. This technique is used most often for—

- Training in human relations skills.

- Training in sensitivity to people and situations.

- Encouraging initiative and self-reliance.

- Stimulating discussion.

- Training in group problem solving.

Among the values of role-playing are the following:

- Individuals can experiment with new ways of behaving.

- Situations and roles may be tailored to individual needs and interests.

- Students can practice real-life situations and risk making mistakes without suffering the consequences of those mistakes.

- Students can observe and analyze more objectively because a role is being played.

- Students can learn by doing.

- Individuals will be more apt to say what they feel rather than what they think another person wants to hear.

- Real-life behavior may be brought into the classroom.

- The potential for training in human interaction skills is unequaled.

When PLANNING a role-playing lesson, the teacher must decide how much structure to give the roles. If the objective is to clarify values or to develop an understanding of another's cultural values, the roles are often left undefined. When the objective is to focus on how individuals function in certain situations (a salesperson handling a customer's objections), the role-playing lesson is more highly structured and the number of optional responses is limited.

Consider using such variations of the technique as the following:

- *Doubling.* One character repeats, raises questions, and thinks along with another actor, but does not contradict.

- *Switching.* At various points, the actors switch roles and continue.

- *Imitation.* One person shows how another played a role.

- *Private thoughts.* An alter ego guesses at what is behind an actor's words.

- *Wheel-leader.* One person in the center of a circle goes around giving the same problem to each participant, each of whom responds immediately. Answers may be tape-recorded and the group may devise a perfected response.

- *Substitution.* The protagonist faces several antagonists to show how people react differently to different people.

To IMPLEMENT this technique, *orientate* the group by describing role-playing, stating the reason(s) for its use, and reducing threat in any way possible. Some effective means of reducing threat include the following reassurances:

- No one will be ridiculed.

- Participants gain the most from the activity.

- People may make mistakes. If they didn't, there would be no need to role-play the situation.

- It's better to make mistakes in the classroom than on the job.

- No one plays him/herself.

In the presentation portion of the *development,* establish the situation, cast the roles, and brief the audience and actors on the situation. Provide only as much information as needed to accomplish the purpose. The briefing session should—

- Include all necessary facts and instructions.

- Be kept to a minimum to allow for spontaneity.

- Be put in writing if at all complicated.

- Aim for reality.

In order to involve the audience as much as possible, the following suggestions may be offered:

- *Be listeners.* Listen for prejudices, voice changes, tempo, hidden motives, assumptions, preconceived ideas.

- *Be watchers.* Watch for body tensions, facial expressions, gestures.

- *Be consultants.* Ask, "How could the situation have been handled differently?"

- *Be empathizers.* Identify with actors and observe by feeling the part.

In the *application* portion, the conditions described in the briefing are acted out. Be perceptive as to when the acting should stop. If the interaction becomes excessively active, consider switching the roles.

Follow-up activities may be numerous, but in all cases a discussion should follow the interaction, in order that key points may be highlighted. The nature of the discussion is dependent upon the objective of the lesson.

To EVALUATE role-playing activities, first look at the stated objective(s). Because student growth in the area of values clarification is difficult to measure even with follow-up studies, however, a more informal and temporal technique is suggested by means of the following questions:

- Did participants understand the roles they were playing?

- Did participants have the background to play the roles?

- Was the activity too long or too short?

- Was the entire class involved either actively or passively?

- Did students feel the relevance of the role-playing activity?

- Would the use of a variation such as doubling have increased learning?

GAMING

Gaming is a way of making learning fun. In free play, children invariably appear to seek out or fabricate ways to compete fairly among themselves or to simulate an agreed-upon segment of their world. Educators can capitalize on this seemingly natural phenomenon by selecting or designing classroom gaming techniques.

Games are basically of two types—the simulation game and the question/answer game. The *simulation game* focuses upon a segment of a societal activity. Through questioning and decision making, the student advances in the activity and, as a result, better understands the dimensions, procedures, and critical conditions encompassed in the game. Although this type is difficult to design, such games have been designed by teachers who are proficient in gaming theory. Since it is beyond the scope of this book, gaming theory will not be discussed here.

The second type, the *question/answer game*, is easier to design and use and is quite adaptable to any subject matter. Rules are patterned after a familiar game such as Jeopardy, baseball, or bingo. Questions may be based on subject materials and originated by the teacher. These games usually result in a winner who is an individual or a team that was more knowledgeable or luckier. In an educational setting it is desirable to have the winning and losing dimension dependent upon knowledge of the subject matter rather than upon chance. If cooperative teams are identified as competitors rather than individuals, students who have difficulty with the subject matter are encouraged to study more so that they contribute more to the team effort. These same students share some of the reward if the team wins. In the event of losing, students who have difficulty with school work are less visible than when they compete on an individual basis.

PLANNING for games is relatively easy. In the case of simulation games, the difficult task is to identify potential games and to select the game that best meets the objectives for the class. Question/answer games, while simple to design, usually require more planning time because the subject matter questions need to be adapted to the format of the game. It is essential that guidelines for sequencing the turns of players and for the resolution of disputes be clear and agreed upon before starting. Once the game planning task is completed, only periodic updating is necessary to keep the questions current and consistent with course objectives.

When IMPLEMENTING a game, little student *orientation* is needed. The activity is self-motivating. It helps students to focus their attention, however, if they know that the game is designed to help them to understand a concept better, to review for a test, or to assist in learning principles and procedures.

In the presentation of this technique, explain the object of the game, the rules, and the procedures for getting started.

During the application, students play the game while the teacher serves as referee, spectator, timer, and/or cheerleader.

Follow-up activities may include a discussion of the concept, a short evaluation of student learning, or a formal test in the near future.

EVALUATION of the gaming technique is direct. Questions such as the following may be asked:

- Were the rules clear and complete?
- Were disputes resolved fairly?
- Did students enjoy the game?
- Did students perform satisfactorily on the test?
- Did the discussion following the game go well?
- Was there enough time to complete the game?

COMMITTEES

A committee is a small group of people who have been identified to perform a task that is too large for an individual or too cumbersome for a larger group. Committees are created to execute one or more defined tasks (e.g., to plan an activity or program, to serve as an advisory board, to study a problem, or to promote an idea or event).

Committee work in the classroom provides many opportunities for the student to develop social skills such as cooperation, leadership, followership, and the power of persuasion. Students learn to participate and to contribute in a self-governing activity which is common and influential in today's society. Many significant contributions are made through local, state, and national committees. When this technique is used in the classroom, students are learning through an effective medium.

Several considerations in PLANNING are essential for the successful use of this interaction technique. Select committee members who are willing to spend the time needed to achieve the goals, who represent a variety of relevant interests, and who work well together. Clearly identify the committee assignment and the work guidelines.

For successful IMPLEMENTATION of this technique, the three-element lesson format is again used. *Orientate* the group by explaining why the objective for the committee was selected and how the committee's recommendations will be used.

To begin the *development,* identify the members of the committee and present all pertinent information concerning their assignment and deadlines. During the *application* portion when the group begins to function, identify or help the members identify a chairperson and secretary.

Informally advise, facilitate, encourage, resolve differences, and/or do anything else that increases the probability of successful committee action. Lastly, after the predetermined time has elapsed, the chairperson reports the group's recommendations which are acted upon in the *follow-up* portion of the lesson. The objective for the committee determines the appropriate action.

EVALUATION is carried out by observing if—

- The committee assignment was adequately identified.

- The committee membership was representative and cooperative.

- Adequate time was provided to accomplish the objectives.

DEBATES

The debate is a pro and con discussion of a question or issue that involves two teams of three to four students, with voluntary participation by the remainder of the class. This T/L technique is an excellent way for the team members to learn about a topic. It is *in*efficient in bringing full understanding to an entire group.

The primary reason for use of this technique is to develop the analytical, communicative, and persuasive skills of the participants.

The following description is of the modified debate which encourages more student interest, voluntary participation, and identification with the topic.

To PLAN the modified technique, take into account the following tasks:

- Introduce the technique, purpose, rules, and procedures of the debate.

- Help students identify a problem that is current, relevant to their daily life, within their range of ability, and that can be researched with available resources.

- Help the class identify teams that have a balance of backgrounds, intelligence, interest, and verbal abilities.

- Set a date for the debate. Provide sufficient time to develop the arguments.

- Provide equal assistance to students on both sides in their researching tasks.

Both the *orientation* and the *development* are included in the preceding planning stage and in the following procedure which may be used to IMPLEMENT the debating technique. The procedure may be shortened by simply omitting certain items. Be sure to retain balance between the sides, however.

- State the problem to both teams.

- Formal presentations:
    Affirmative—five minutes
    Negative—five minutes

- Rebuttals: Affirmative—five minutes
                Negative—five minutes

- Questions/contributions from floor:
    Affirmative
    Negative
    (Repeat as needed. Keep sides balanced.)

- Open to audience for speeches or to ask questions of speakers. (Balance both sides.)

- Summary speakers:
    Affirmative—three minutes
    Negative—three minutes

- Open to ask questions of speakers or audience. (Balance both sides.)

- Summarize and categorize new information. (Teacher)

It is recommended that the formal presentations, rebuttals, and summaries by the affirmative and negative sides be limited to one-half of the class period. The remainder of the class time may be used as a *follow-up* in which to discuss the topic, the debating technique, the success of the team members in supporting their point of view, and additional activities to build upon the ideas brought out in the debate.

EVALUATE the technique by asking the following questions:

- Did the class (audience) participate freely?

- Were both sides of the topic well presented?

- Was the discussion from the floor balanced between the affirmative and negative positions?

- Were the objectives of developing analytical, communicative, and persuasive skills achieved?

SUMMARY

Interaction techniques are most valuable in developing affective, communicative, and interpersonal skills. They are less valuable when the goal is to develop cognitive skills and psychomotor skills. These techniques attempt to tap a rich reservoir of natural talent possessed by most young people—the talent to exchange ideas at an accelerated rate. To let such a resource go unused would be extremely wasteful, particularly when such effective methods of channeling and developing these abilities are so readily available in the classroom.

Chapter 9.

OTHER METHODS OF PROVIDING MEANINGFUL VARIETY
(Determining the Working Conditions)

Purpose: Furniture designer/builders receive requests to build single items or multiple items, to build to customer's specifications or to their own. They also have the option to compete or to cooperate in the marketplace. Teachers, on the other hand, do not have the luxury of selecting the conditions under which they operate when they want to maximize learning. They need to understand their options therefore and how to apply them; they also need to be flexible enough to respond effectively to conditions when necessary. This chapter introduces methods of managing the class organization, teacher/student dominance, and goal structures for the purpose of maximizing learning. Teacher flexibility is the key.

Objective: When you have finished this chapter, you will understand the options available in class organization, teacher/student dominance, and goal structures so that you can make recommendations for a strategy to use in a given T/L situation.

As stated earlier, no single T/L technique is effective with all students or with all content. In fact, even if all such techniques were perfectly implemented, their effectiveness would still be limited. Certain student characteristics and intended outcomes cannot be accommodated until other adjustments in the instructional strategy are made. These variations are related to the social environment in which instruction occurs. Teachers can make finer adjustments to the learner and to the content by varying (1) the class organization, (2) the teacher/student dominance in the selection of objectives and learning strategy, and (3) the goal structures employed in the classroom.

VARYING THE CLASS ORGANIZATION

Teachers can provide meaningful variety by changing the size of the group working on a particular objective. Group sizes may range from one person to the entire class. Many students have preferences about the number of people on a work team. Some prefer to work alone, others prefer to work in groups of two to five, and still others may prefer to be a part of a group of ten to twenty-five students.

Another factor affecting the ideal group size is the objective to be achieved. If the objective concerns the understanding of the physical principle describing the mechanical advantage of simple machines, for example, students may learn about this individually, in subgroups, or in a large group. Student preference would be the determiner. If, however, the objective is to develop cooperative work habits, leadership, or interpersonal skills, work in subgroups or large groups is necessary to provide practice in cooperating, leading, and interacting.

Another dimension of class organization is the number of students who are expected to achieve any one objective. Does each student have individual goals or are all students working toward the same objective? If the subject matter for the segment of instruction does not consist of basic skills and does not need to be articulated with a subsequent course, students may choose their own objectives. Conversely, if the subject matter consists of competencies that must be mastered by each student in order to receive credit, the objectives may be the same for all students. Of course, other possible situations may occur at any point between the extremes of individual and group objectives.

Figure 5 is included to assist in visualizing the relationship between the two variables.

	Subgroup	Full Group
Full-Group Objectives	A	B	C
Individual Objectives	D	E (Uncommon)	F (Uncommon)

| | Subgroup | Full Group |

Figure 5.

CLASS ORGANIZATION IN RELATION TO OBJECTIVES AND GROUP SIZE

The matrix displays four options from which teachers may select. Options E and F are uncommon. The preferences of students and the nature of the content are the contributing factors in making selections. A brief description of each option should help to better understand the variables.

Option A: Individuals work on group objectives (standard objectives but individually paced work).

Option B: Small groups work on group objectives (standard objectives but students are grouped by aptitude or personal preferences).

Option C: Full group works on group objectives (standard objectives and group activities with group deadlines).

Option D: Individuals work on individual objectives. Students identify the objectives and set their own pace.

Option E: Individuals work on individual objectives but stay in subgroup (an uncommon option).

Option F: Individuals work on individual and group objectives (an uncommon option).

VARYING TEACHER/STUDENT DOMINANCE

The term *teacher/student dominance* refers to the degree and kind of teacher/student involvement in selecting the objectives and the learning strategy used to achieve the objectives. In discussions of principles or conditions of learning, most educators maintain that students who participate in the selection of the objectives and learning strategy are more highly motivated than those who do not participate. Figure 6 illustrates the teacher/student dominance phenomenon.

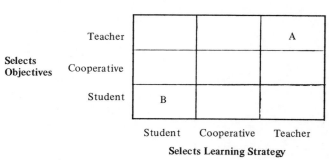

Figure 6.

TEACHER/STUDENT DOMINANCE IN SELECTING OBJECTIVES AND LEARNING STRATEGY

The degree of teacher/student dominance ranges from total teacher domination (A) to total student domination (B), although these extremes in the continuum are highly uncommon. Research in this area indicates that—

- Teacher-dominated behavior such as demanding, assigning, and belittling student efforts leads to apathy, withdrawal, and hostility toward self and teacher.

- Student-dominated behavior which includes teacher acceptance and support and the use of known criteria to constructively evaluate or criticize student work leads to lower anxiety levels and to emotionally stable and cooperative behavior.

The degree to which objectives are considered basic skills (spelling, reading, computing, or speaking) and the degree to which they are articulated with other objectives will determine the amount of flexibility allowed in student selection. In other words, the more the objectives are considered "basic," the less flexibility in student selection. The level of student independence and security will also help the teacher in deciding how much involvement the student desires or can tolerate. The more independent and secure the student, the more she/he may participate in decisions.

When identified by students, the objective should be stated in performance terms. Students may assist in selecting the observable behavior, the level of performance, the conditions, and the method used to evaluate the objective. The strategy decision involves selecting the T/L techniques, the sequence (including deadlines), the environment, and the persons and resources to be consulted.

VARYING THE GOAL STRUCTURE

The goal structure describes the kind of interdependence existing among students; it also describes the teacher/student relationship in achieving instructional aims. The four kinds of goal structures are the following:

1. *Interpersonal Competition*

Although competition may have potentially destructive effects, under certain conditions the use of interpersonal competition can be advantageous—when, for example:

- It helps to increase student performance on simple drill activities.
- The level of anxiety is kept low during the competion.
- The only criterion for evaluating student performance is to compare it to the performance of another.
- Scoring of the competition is visible.
- Students think they have a chance of winning (i.e., they are well matched in ability).
- Procedures for resolving disagreements and determining winners are clearly explained.

2. *Intergroup Competition*

Intergroup competition is a way to cushion the disappointment of losing, to develop cohesiveness in a group, and to increase the interaction between high achievers and underachievers. In this structure teams are formed. If the team loses, the loss will have less negative effect on the individuals within the group than if they were separate competitors because the loss is suffered by the team rather than by individuals.

Members of this group structure are cohesive because they have a single goal with which each member identifies and to which each member contributes. When low achievers are members of the group, high achievers are more likely to help them perform better which also enables the team to do better in the competion.

3. *Cooperative Structure*

In a cooperative atmosphere, students are organized around achieving a single goal with no competition involved. Cooperative goal structures are recommended when the instructional aim is to develop group problem-solving skills, group decision-making skills, and values clarification.

4. *Individualistic Structure*

In the individualistic structure, students compete against themselves in an effort to achieve their reward or goal. These goal structures are selected to develop a specific skill or understanding when assignments are clear and when students need extra help.

SUMMARY

This chapter discussed four useful options for organizing a class, several recommendations in the area of teacher/student dominance, and four goal structures. In addition, suggestions were made for the implementation of these methods of providing meaningful variety in the learning environment. With this background of information, it is hoped that teacher planning will be facilitated and that the implementation of these methods will enable students to learn more effectively and enjoyably.

EPILOGUE

The analogy of the furniture builder and the teacher was adequate to make on-the-surface comparisons—to illustrate some rather abstract ideas with a familiar, concrete example. To interpret teaching as being as easily controlled and as predictable as building furniture, however, would be misleading.

For example, teachers seldom first select the objectives and then select the students who have the greatest potential for achieving them. Furniture builders, on the other hand, do just that. They determine the specifications; then and only then is the material selected. Reversing the procedure by responsible woodworkers is practically unheard of.

The second difference relates to the degree of control of the furniture builder and the teacher over the uniformity and quality of their materials. When lumber is ordered, it is ordered by grade which insures that a specified level of quality and uniformity in the moisture content, species, defects, and size is maintained. Teachers have little control over the quality of students with whom they work. Students in the classroom vary in size, educational background, interests, goals, temperament, and many other characteristics. If furniture builders were confronted with such a degree of variability in their materials, the consistency of quality in their finished product would vary considerably.

The third major difference communicated by the analogy is that T/L techniques and procedures are highly predictable. Close tolerances on dimensions can be held over thousands of repetitions of an operation with woodworking equipment. The tools and procedures of teaching (T/L techniques and lesson plans) are not nearly so predictable.

The fact that teachers must adapt to many variables significantly complicates the task of carrying on effective instruction. One way to reduce the effects of the variables and to increase effectiveness is to provide meaningful variety.

If several different T/L techniques are selected in response to a diverse student body, the variety gains in meaning. If an assortment of instructional objectives is learned with different and appropriate techniques, the variety takes on additional meaning. By adjusting the techniques to respond to class and activity schedules in the school day, even greater meaning is given the variety. Finally, maximum meaning is assigned variety when teachers are knowledgeable and flexible enough to select the best group size, teacher/student dominance, and goal structure to provide the most interesting and effective instruction possible. By maximizing meaningful variety, success in the classroom is also maximized.

APPENDIX

SAMPLE LESSON PLANS

Code for Instructional Materials

C: Chart

FS: Filmstrip

G: Game

HO: Handout

M: Model

MP: Motion Picture

O: Object

OT: Overhead Transparency

P: Picture

LESSON PLAN

UNIT _____

LESSON TITLE _____

OBJECTIVES   At the conclusion of this lesson the student should be able to—

REFERENCES

TEACHER ACTIVITY

Equipment

Materials

STUDENT ACTIVITY

Equipment

Materials

CONTENT AND PROCEDURES

I.   Orientation

II. Development

    A. Presentation

    B. Application

III. Follow-up

LESSON PLAN—*Lecture (Little Method),*
Brainstorming, and Debate

UNIT _____ Presenting Controversial Issues _____

LESSON TITLE _____ Using Debates _____

OBJECTIVES   At the conclusion of this lesson (in two or three weeks), the
student should be able to—

1. Describe briefly what debates are, reasons for conducting them, and
    methods of conducting them.
2. Identify a topic, take sides, prepare for, and conduct a debate on a
    topic.

REFERENCES

TEACHER ACTIVITY

Equipment

Materials

STUDENT ACTIVITY

Equipment

Materials

CONTENT AND PROCEDURES

I. Orientation
   A. Do you think a teacher should paddle a student?
   B. Short discussion.
   C. Controversial issues are often debated.
   D. We will learn this skill.

II. Development
   A. Presentation
      1. What is a debate?
         a. Organize
         b. Present pro/con of issue
         c. Equal representation
         d. Initial presentation
         e. Rebuttals
         f. Discussion
      2. Why debate?
         a. Present both sides of issue
         b. Fair representation
         c. Individuals decide on view
      3. How to prepare for a debate
         a. Interview knowledgeable people
         b. Research articles in periodicals
         c. Prepare position speech
         d. Prepare rebuttal

   B. Application
      1. Identify topic: Use brainstorming
         a. State any interesting topic
            —All topics are good
            —No negative comments
         b. List ideas on board
         c. Each student chooses five topics
         d. Select topic (vote)
      2. Students choose pro/con side (try to keep sides even)
      3. Students select three for team
      4. Prepare for debate (two weeks)
         a. Entire group participates
         b. Use research techniques (individually)
         c. Group meets to compare notes
      5. Conduct debate (in class period)
       (teams of three in front across table)
         a. Presentation speech: Pro (3-5 min.)
         b. Presentation speech: Con (3-5 min.)
         c. Rebuttal: Pro (3-5 min.)
         d. Rebuttal: Con (3-5 min.)
         e. Ask audience to contribute (2 min. maximum)

III. Follow-up
   A. Write brief summary of views
   B. Give constructive criticism to team

LESSON PLAN—*Lecture (Parable)*

UNIT _____ Modern Survival _____

LESSON TITLE __A Cheap Bicycle_____

OBJECTIVES   At the conclusion of this lesson, students should be able, when divided into pairs, to—

1.   List three elements necessary for survival.
2.   From memory, list three causes of high prices.
3.   State three methods of decreasing survival costs.

REFERENCES

TEACHER ACTIVITY

Equipment

Overhead projector

Materials

OT: A Need Indeed!
OT: Demand's Command

STUDENT ACTIVITY

Equipment

Materials

HO: What We Need
HO: Simplifying Survival

CONTENT AND PROCEDURES

I. Orientation—Aim (HO: What We Need)
    A.   Understand how survival costs rise
    B.   Learn the steps that might reduce survival costs

II. Development
    A.   Presentation
        1.   Analogy: *Paying for survival is like buying a bicycle*
        2.   Description of detail
            a.   Plan/select bicycle (OT: A Need Indeed)
               —Why the need?
               —Who is buying
               —Sorority Sue
               —President Peter
               —Leisure Lou
               —Congressperson Blue
               —Unemployed Ed
               —The cost?
               —Money
               —Supply
               —Demand
            b.   Implement buying a bicycle (OT: Demand's Command)
               —The bidding
               —The price
            c.   Evaluate: Was it a good choice?
               —Did bicycle meet needs?
               —Was cost fair?
               —Ways to reduce cost
    B.   Application (HO: Simplifying Survival)
        1.   Divide into pairs
        2.   Identify any three elements of survival
        3.   List three causes of cost increase for one element
        4.   List three methods of element reduction

III. Follow-up
    A.   Identify a necessity at home (one of the utilities, clothes, transportation)
    B.   Plan ways to reduce your "survival costs"
    C.   Describe your plan in a written paper no longer than two pages
    D.   Implement as much of the plan as you can
    E.   Evaluate the success and problems of the plan

LESSON PLAN—*Informal Lecture and
Guided Observation*

UNIT ____Laminating Wood_____

LESSON TITLE ___Defining Terms_____

OBJECTIVES   At the conclusion of this lesson, the student should be able—

1. When given ten consecutively numbered examples illustrating the six kinds of wood assemblies, to match the number on the example with the term on a response form with 100% accuracy.

2. When asked at random, to verbally distinguish between lamination in general, wood lamination, and plywood. (A correct answer will include the key terms in the handout.)

REFERENCES

TEACHER ACTIVITY

Equipment

Opaque projector
Overhead projector

Materials

OT: Lamination Is. . .
 P: Eames chair
 P: Laminated beam
 O: Bent wood chair
 O: Solid wood sample
 O: 2 layers of veneer (6" x 6")
 O: Badminton racket
 O: Laminated fabric sample
 O: Painted board
 O: Plated pipe

STUDENT ACTIVITY

Equipment

Materials

      Observation Response Form
 10   examples of six processes
  2   solid wood
  1   flat lamination
  2   bent wood laminations
  2   flat plywood
  2   molded plywood
  1   laminated picture
  1   bent wood
HO: Lamination Is. . .

CONTENT AND PROCEDURES

I. Orientation—Purposes
    A.   Clarify terms
        1.   Lamination has several definitions
        2.   Facilitate communication
    B.   Understand variables involved

II. Development
    A.   Presentation
        1.   Lamination Is. . .(OT and HO)
            a.   Definition
            b.   Examples
                —Positive: laminated picture and cloth
                —Negative: painted board and plated pipe
        2.   Terms defined
            a.   Solid wood (on handout)
            b.   Bent wood (on handout)
            c.   Flat lamination (on handout)
            d.   Wood lamination (on handout)
                —Illustrate (use questions)
                      Use two layers of veneer
                      Change orientation
            e.   Flat plywood lamination (on handout)
                —Illustrate (use questions)
                      Use two layers of veneer
                      Change orientation
                —Examples: plywood samples
            f.   Bent wood lamination (on handout)
                —Illustrate (use questions)
                      Use two layers of veneer
                      Change orientation
                      Bend them
                —Example: beams in building and badminton racket
            g.   Molded plywood lamination (on handout)
                —Illustrate (use questions)
                      Hold up variety of positive and negative examples.
                      Examples: Eames chair
    B.   Application
        1.   Handout response forms
        2.   Go over instructions
            a.   Ten numbered examples
            b.   Identify process used
            c.   Place number next to process
            d.   Assign students to pairs
            e.   Circulate among examples
            f.   Discuss answers
            g.   Use handouts
        3.   Begin

III. Follow-up
    A.   Go over answers; discuss differences
    B.   Ask students to define each term

DEFINING LAMINATION AND RELATED TERMS

1. **solid wood**. A single piece of wood.

2. **lamination**. An assembly consisting of two or more layers of solid material joined together with an adhesive.

3. **wood lamination**. A flat assembly consisting of two or more pieces of wood joined with an adhesive with grains parallel.

4. **plywood lamination**. A flat assembly consisting of two or more layers of wood joined with an adhesive with grains crossed.

5. **bent wood lamination**. A curved assembly consisting of two or more layers of wood joined with an adhesive. Grains are parallel and layers are bent to fit a curved form.

6. **molded plywood**. A curved assembly consisting of two or more layers of wood joined with adhesives. Grains are crossed and layers bent to fit a curved form.

OBSERVATION RESPONSE FORM

INSTRUCTIONS: Look at the sample and place the letter that describes the sample in the blank that is numbered the same as the sample.

1. _____   A.   lamination

2. _____   B.   flat wood lamination

3. _____   C.   flat plywood lamination

4. _____   D.   bent wood lamination

5. _____   E.   molded plywood lamination

6. _____   F.   solid wood

7. _____   G.   bent solid wood

8. _____

9. _____

10. _____

LESSON PLAN—*Guest Lecturer*

UNIT _____ Careers in Home Economics _____

LESSON TITLE __ Overview of Careers _____

OBJECTIVES   At the conclusion of this lesson the student should be able, when given one week, to use six characteristics of careers to describe a career or career cluster in the area of home economics.

REFERENCES

TEACHER ACTIVITY

Equipment

Materials

STUDENT ACTIVITY

Equipment

Materials

CONTENT AND PROCEDURES

I. Orientation
    A.   We have been studying:
        1.   Preparing meals
        2.   Buying and producing cloth products
        3.   Using household equipment
    B.   Tomorrow we learn about careers in the field

II. Development (prior to guest lecture)
    A.   Presentation
        1.   Ms. _____ will visit
        2.   Specialist in careers in home economics
        3.   Describe the following
            a.   Range of occupations
            b.   Preparation
            c.   General duties in careers
            d.   Working conditions
            e.   Rewards
            f.   Personal requirements
    B.   Application
        1.   Take list in II. A. 3 to neighbor, parent, other teacher
            a.   Ask questions relevant to these points (in II. A. 3)
            b.   Develop specific questions to ask guest
        2.   Bring minimum of two specific questions to class

III. Development (day of guest lecture)
    A.   Preparation
        1.   Introduction
            a.   Ms. _____ is here from _____
            b.   She is an Extension Home Economist.
            c.   Discuss careers in home economics
            d.   Make formal remarks
            e.   Available for questions
            f.   Write down questions as you listen
    B.   Application
        1.   Students have some questions
        2.   Raise hands
            a.   Ask questions
            b.   Discuss points of confusion
        3.   Stop
            a.   When questions stop or
            b.   Five minutes before bell

IV. Follow-up
    A.   Thank Ms. _____ for coming
    B.   Assignment
        1.   Options
            a.   Report: Four handwritten pages
            b.   Display: to fit bulletin board
            c.   Presentation: three minutes in length
        2.   Topic: Career or Career Cluster in Home Economics
        3.   Due one week from today
        4.   Include items in II. A. 3

LESSON PLAN—*Demonstration (Manipulative Skill) and Experiment*

UNIT   Molecules of Life

LESSON TITLE   Identifying Carbohydrates

OBJECTIVES   At the conclusion of this lesson, when given three unknown food samples, test equipment, test indicator solutions, and procedures, the student should be able to—

1. Conduct the experiment.
2. Correctly identify each unknown food sample.

REFERENCES

TEACHER ACTIVITY

Equipment

1	beaker (250 ml)
6	test tubes
1	hot plate
2	droppers

Materials

Benedict's solution
1% glucose solution
Iodine solution
1% starch solution
Egg white
Biuret solution

STUDENT ACTIVITY

Equipment

1 beaker (250 ml)
3 test tubes
1 hot plate
2 droppers

Materials

Food sample 1
Food sample 2
Food sample 3
Benedict's solution
Iodine solution
Biuret solution
3 Laboratory Data Sheets

CONTENT AND PROCEDURES

I. Orientation
   A.   Verify readings
   B.   Learn chemical analysis procedures
   C.   Analyze common foods

II. Development
   A.   Presentation
       1.   Demonstration: Identifying sugar
          a.   Prepare specimens
             —Put two drops water in one test tube
             —Put two drops glucose in another test tube
          b.   Heat both specimens in water bath to 100° C
          c.   Add three drops Benedict's solution to each
          d.   Observe color change
             —blue to yellow
             —red to brown
       2.   Demonstration: Identifying starch
          a.   Prepare specimens
             —Put two drops water in one test tube
             —Put two drops starch in another test tube
          b.   Heat both specimens in water bath to 100° C
          c.   Add two drops iodine solution to each
          d.   Observe black in starch
       3.   Demonstration: Identifying protein
          a.   Prepare specimens
             —Put two drops water in one test tube
             —Put two drops egg yolk in another test tube
          b.   Heat both specimens in water to 100° C
          c.   Add two drops Biuret solution to each
          d.   Observe purple in egg yolk

   B.   Application
       1.   Given
          a.   Three food samples
          b.   Three laboratory data sheets
          c.   Teams of two
       2.   Procedure
          a.   Prepare three specimens of each sample (label)
          b.   Add three drops of test solution (label)

Samples

	1	2	3
Benedict's			
Iodine			
Biuret			

          c.   Observe colors
          d.   Complete laboratory data sheets

III. Follow-up
   A.   Review findings and conclusions

LESSON PLAN—*Demonstration (Physical*
Principle)

UNIT _____ Laminating Wood _____

LESSON TITLE _____ Definitions—Grain _____

OBJECTIVES   At the conclusion of this lesson, the student should be able—

1. When asked at random, to state two methods of identifying grain direction.

2. When given pieces of wood, to determine the grain direction 100% of the time.

3. When asked at random, to verbally describe how grain direction influences the strength of wood. A correct answer will include a comparison between breaks "with" and "across" the grain.

REFERENCES

TEACHER ACTIVITY

Equipment

Materials

O: 15 soda straws
O: 1 note pad
O: 1 pine (3/4" x 2" x 8")
O: 1 pine (3/4" x 8" x 2")
O: 20 pieces of veneer (3" x 3")
O: 1 laminated candle holder
O: 1 stirring rod (solid wood)
O: 1 softwood (2" x 4" x 15")
O: 1 particle board (3/4" x 3" x 12")

STUDENT ACTIVITY

Equipment

Materials

CONTENT AND PROCEDURES

I. Orientation
   A.   Wood has some special characteristics
   B.   Influence on its use

II. Development
   A.   Presentation
      1.   How wood is constructed
         a.   Made of cells
            —Long
            —Narrow
            —Like closed-ended soda straws
         b.   Cells joined
            —Lignin in wood
            —Wax in soda straws
         c.   Tear piece of paper
            —See the fuzzies
            —Individual cells
      2.   How its construction influences strength of wood
         a.   Put 3/4" x 2" x 12" wood in vise
         b.   Would you break this?
         c.   Put 3/4" x 12" x 2" wood in vise
         d.   Break this one
         e.   Find any differences?
         f.   Handout veneer samples
         g.   Break them with and across grain
         h.   Find any difference?
         i.   What is the direction of the grain?
   B.   Application: Analyze why the grain in several wood products goes in the direction it does

III. Follow-up
   A.   Why is the grain direction important when you make something of wood?
   B.   How can you tell the direction of the grain?

LESSON PLAN—*Demonstration (Mechanical Device)*

UNIT _____ Distributing Your Ideas

LESSON TITLE _____ "Spirit Duplicator"

OBJECTIVES   At the conclusion of this lesson, the student should be able—

1. Without the aid of references and when called upon at random, to list three of the seven parts of the spirit duplicator and to describe the function of each.

2. With the use of notes, to set up, run copies, and shut down the spirit duplicator without making an error.

REFERENCES

Brown, Lewis, and Harcleroad. *Audio-Visual Instruction: Technology, Media, and Methods.* pp. 509-11.

TEACHER ACTIVITY

Equipment

Spirit duplicator (ready to run)
Motion picture projector (Super 8)

Materials

C: Spirit duplicator parts
25 sheets of ditto paper
 1 spirit master
MP: *Making Spirit Duplicator Masters*

STUDENT ACTIVITY

Equipment

Materials

CONTENT AND PROCEDURES

I. Orientation
   A.   All schools have them
   B.   Most common duplicating process
   C.   Objective
      1.   Describe operation
      2.   Run copies

II. Development
   A. Presentation
      1.   Parts and functions
         a.   Feed wheels: start page
         b.   Moistening roller: coats paper with fluid
         c.   Forward roller: advances paper
         d.   Master: image carrier
         e.   Impression roller: applies pressure
         f.   Stop: helps stack copies
      2.   Relationship
         a.   Feed wheels start and pace feed
         b.   1(b), (c), (d), and (e) connected with direct drive and uniformly timed
      3.   Operation
         a.   Ready duplicator
            —Check fluid in tank
            —Adjust paper gripper and guides
            —Set pressure lever to "1"
            —Set fluid tank to fill reservoir
         b.   Attach master
            —Put handle at 6:00
            —Open clamp lever
            —Insert top edge of master (carbon up)
            —Return clamp lever
            —Crease master
         c.   Run copies
            —Turn handle, each turn in one copy
            —Check location on page, adjust if necessary
            —Check image darkness
            —Adjust pressure if necessary
            —Run number needed
         d.   Remove master
            —Put handle at 6:00
            —Open clamp
            —Lift out master
            —Set pressure to "O"
            —Raise feed wheel
            —Turn fluid tank with nozzle up
            —Replace dust cover
CAUTION: Avoid contact of fluid on skin; avoid breathing excessive fumes
   B.   Application
      1.   Point to parts and ask names
      2.   Have students provide steps to set up the machine
      3.   Have students in groups of two set up machine and run five copies of the machine parts and procedures

III. Follow-up
   A.   Watch the film *Making Spirit Duplicator Masters*
   B.   Make a handmade master
   C.   Run it

LESSON PLAN—*Audiovisuals*

UNIT   Molecules of Life

LESSON TITLE   Atomic Structure

OBJECTIVES   At the conclusion of this lesson, the student should be able—

1. When asked at random, to define atoms, ions, and molecules.
2. When given equipment and materials and number of electrons, protons, and neutrons, to draw correctly a model of an atom.
3. When shown nine models of atoms, to determine correctly if they are positive, negative, or neutral.

REFERENCES

Biology, Smallwood and Green, chapter 3, "The Molecules of Life"

TEACHER ACTIVITY

Equipment

Filmstrip projector

Materials

Crayons
Paper
M: 3 + atoms
M: 3 - atoms
M: 3 neutral atoms

STUDENT ACTIVITY

Equipment

Scissors

Materials

Crayons
Paper

CONTENT AND PROCEDURES

I. Orientation
  A. Pyramids built of stone
  B. Buildings made of brick and boards
  C. Clothes made of fibers
  D. What is matter made of?
     (Atoms, ions, and molecules)

II. Development
  A. Presentation
     1. Going to see a filmstrip
     2. Look for:
        a. Parts of an atom
        b. What is an ion?
        c. What are molecules?
     3. Show first fourteen frames of filmstrip

  B. Application
     1. Use paper, crayons, and scissors to make paper model of atoms and molecules
        a. Nitrogen atom
        b. Lithium atom
        c. Water molecules

III. Follow-up
  A. Questions
     1. What are the parts of an atom?
     2. What is an ion?
     3. What are molecules?

  B. Determine if the following models are +, -, or neutral (show models of each).

LESSON PLAN—*Committee*

UNIT _____ (Fits most subject areas) _____

LESSON TITLE _____ Planning a Field Trip _____

OBJECTIVES   At the conclusion of this lesson, students should be able, when asked at random, to—

1.   List their representatives.
2.   Describe the duties of the chairperson and secretary.
3.   Describe their task.
4.   State the deadline.

REFERENCES

TEACHER ACTIVITY

Equipment

Materials

STUDENT ACTIVITY

Equipment

Materials

CONTENT AND PROCEDURES

I. Orientation
  A. Students help decide on field trip
  B. Many interesting places to visit

II. Development
  A. Presentation
    1. Half- or full-day field trip
    2. School to pay transportation
    3. Maximum fifty miles one way
    4. Students provide meals
    5. Committee represents class
  B. Application
    1. Committee
      a. Class president
      b. Vice-president
      c. Treasurer
      d. Two elected members
    2. Organize committee
      a. Select chairperson
        —Schedule meeting
        —Conduct meeting
        —Report committee action
        —Conduct class discussions
      b. Select secretary (to keep minutes)
    3. Task of the committee
      a. Identify field trip site
      b. Set date
      c. Plan day's schedule
      d. Estimate cost
      e. Collect fees
    4. Timetable: two to three weeks for planning

III. Follow-up
  A. Who are your representatives?
  B. What are the duties of officers?
  C. What is your task?
  D. When must you complete task?

LESSON PLAN—*Project (Producer)*

UNIT _____Desserts_____

LESSON TITLE _____Battle of the Sexes Pie Bake-Off_____

OBJECTIVES   At the conclusion of this lesson, the student should be able—

1. When asked at random, to state the rules for the "Pie Bake-Off" without error.
2. When given two 55-minute "pie labs" on fruit and custard pies and two additional 55-minute periods, to produce a pie that earns forty-five points.

REFERENCES

Crocker, B. *New Picture Cook Book,* pp. 335-62

TEACHER ACTIVITY

Equipment

Supply table

Materials

Flour
Salt
Shortening
O: 1 double crust lattice-top cherry pie
O: 1 single crust pecan pie
O: 1 pie shell (lemon meringue pie)

STUDENT ACTIVITY

Equipment

Kitchen utensils

Materials

Standard crust ingredients

CONTENT AND PROCEDURES

I. Orientation
  A. "Battle of the Sexes Pie Bake-Off"
  B. Prizes
    1. Winners are served the pies
    2. Winners don't have to wash dishes

II. Development
  A. Presentation
    1. Rules
      a. Eligibility
        —Enrolled in Basic Home Economics
        —Completed two "pie labs"
      b. Recipe specifications: your choice
        —Standard crust ingredients provided
        —Contestant provides filling
        —Contestant provides nonstandard ingredients
        —Must be made in two 55-minute periods
      c. Making the pie
        —Begin next Monday
        —Take two periods
      d. Judging: Wednesday
        —Determining winners
            average scores for each sex
            highest average wins
        —Panel of four judges
            1 other home economics teacher
            1 other teacher
            1 parent (not of contestant)
            1 student-selected judge
        —Judging scale
            Appearance . . . . 10 points
            Pastry . . . . 10 points
            Flavor . . . . 10 points
            Creativity . . . . 15 points
            Degree of difficulty . . . . . . 5 points
  B. Application
    1. Submit name for fourth judge
    2. Select recipe
      a. Divide into kitchen groups
      b. Read three recipes
      c. Copy one to be made
      d. Make lab plans

III. Follow-up
  A. Who is eligible?
  B. When do we make the pies?
  C. How are the pies judged?

LESSON PLAN—*Project (Problem Solving)*

UNIT _____ Budgeting Your Resources _____

LESSON TITLE _____ Planning a Vacation _____

OBJECTIVES   At the conclusion of this lesson, students should be able, when given a fictitious $600 and twelve days, to—

1. Budget their time.
2. Budget their money.
3. Visit places that interest them most.
4. Write an interesting and informative report.

REFERENCES

    Encyclopedias
    Brochures
    Road maps
    Atlas

TEACHER ACTIVITY

Equipment

Overhead projector

Materials

OT: Maps
OT: Daily Log

STUDENT ACTIVITY

Equipment

Materials

HO: Daily Log
HO: Folder Outline

CONTENT AND PROCEDURES

I. Orientation
  A. Tie-in with previous lessons
    1. "Check-writing" lesson
    2. Reading maps
    3. Writing business letters
    4. Reading reference materials
  B. How can we get the most from our time and our money?

II. Development
  A. Presentation
    1. Resources
      a. Mode of transportation
      b. Companions
      c. Time
      d. Money
    2. Plan how to use resources
      a. Where to go
      b. Points of interest
      c. Do as many things as you can
      d. Describe your trip in a folder (HO: Folder Outline)
  B. Application
    1. Resources
      a. $600
      b. Twelve days
      c. Car (20 mpg @ $.99/gal.)
      d. Companions (from none to two)
    2. Trip description
      a. Daily Log (copy attached)
      b. Outline map of states visited (HO: Folder Outline)
      c. Reports (one for each state)
        —Explain activities
        —Describe points of interest
        —Describe capitol city
    3. Techniques
      a. Talk with students, parents, and companions
      b. Go to libraries
      c. Read brochures
    4. Completion date (three weeks from today)
    5. Grading folders*
      a. Each log
      b. Map
      c. Each report (four best)
      d. Table of contents
      e. Cover of folder

III. Follow-up: Share with others
  A. Describe a point of interest
  B. Summarize the trip

*Teachers should feel free to vary the weighting and to establish the criteria to use with each of the five areas graded.

DAILY LOG

Month _____ Day _____, 19_____

Drove _____ miles today.

Drove for _____ hours_____ minutes today.

Driven _____ miles so far.

Spent $ _____ for breakfast.

Spent $ _____ for lunch.

Spent $ _____ for dinner.

Stopped at _____ for _____ hour(s).

Cost was $ _____.

Stayed in _____ tonight.

Spent $ _____ for lodging.

Spent $ _____ for gasoline today.

Total spent today $ _____ .

Total spent to date $ _____.

Amount of money left $ _____ .

FOLDER OUTLINE

I. Draw Outline Map

    A. Decide which states you plan to visit.
    B. Chart your route, using atlas.
    C. Illustrate points of interest.
    D. Label cities where you lodge.

II. Daily Logs

    A. Determine mileage.
    B. Determine gasoline expenses.
    C. Determine food and lodging expenses.
    D. Determine amount of money left.

III. Written Reports

    A. Use encyclopedias.
    B. Use brochures.

IV. Table of Contents

V. Cover for Folder

LESSON PLAN—*Project (Specific Skill)*

UNIT _____ Writing a Position Paper _____

LESSON TITLE _____ The Project _____

OBJECTIVES   At the conclusion of this lesson, the student should be able to—

1. Find the data.
2. When asked at random, describe the project by including:
    a. Length
    b. Number of passengers to save
    c. Justification of selection
    d. Due date.

REFERENCES

(The source of the problem has been lost. I am grateful to its author and apologize for not giving him/her credit.)

TEACHER ACTIVITY

Equipment

Materials

STUDENT ACTIVITY

Equipment

Materials

HO: Plane Crash Dilemma (see p. 93)

CONTENT AND PROCEDURES

I. Orientation
    A. Prepare position paper
    B. Use imagination
    C. Clarify values

II. Development
    A. Presentation
        1. Plane crash in ocean (HO: Plane Crash Dilemma)
        2. Only one life raft
            a. Twelve will survive
            b. Fifteen will perish
        3. Select the survivors
        4. Decide why they were selected
        5. And/or decide why certain ones perished
    B. Application
        1. Write position paper
            a. 500-600 words
            b. Handwritten and legible
        2. Justify choices
        3. Due in two days
        4. Discuss decisions

III. Follow-up
    A. How long is the paper?
    B. What is included?
    C. How many survived?
    D. How many perished?
    E. When is paper due?

LESSON PLAN—*Exercise*

UNIT ____Laminating Wood_____

LESSON TITLE Identifying and Using Molds_____

OBJECTIVES   At the conclusion of this lesson, the student should be able—

1.   When shown variations of "matched" molds and "one-peice" molds, to categorize them into the two categories without error.
2.   When asked at random, to state one advantage or one disadvantage of each kind of mold.
3.   When given printed instructions, materials, equipment, and fifty-five minutes, to successfully make one part with the assigned mold.

REFERENCES

TEACHER ACTIVITY

Equipment

1 set flat plywood molds
1 set matched molds
1 inflatable mold
1 detergent bottle mold and rubber
   bands
1 ring mold

Materials

Sufficient veneer cut to fit each mold

STUDENT ACTIVITY

Equipment

3 jug molds with rubber bans
3 detergent bottle molds and rubber
   bands
3 ring molds
3 sets matched molds

Materials

 6 sets two-part adhesives
 3 matched mold instructions
 3 ring mold instructions
 3 rubber band mold instructions
12 1" brushes

CONTENT AND PROCEDURES

I. Orientation
   A. The mold determines the shape of the part
   B. Many different kinds
   C. Some very inexpensive
   D. Objectives
      1. Determine purpose of molds
      2. Describe kinds of molds
      3. Use the molds

II. Development
   A. Presentation
      1. Purpose of molds
         a. Determine shape
         b. Provide clamping surface
         c. Hold layers together while adhesive hardens
      2. Components of mold
         a. Rigid surface
         b. Pressure device
      3. Kinds of molds
         a. Matched molds: two rigid pressing surfaces
            —Produce parts fast
            —Exert uniform pressure
            —Difficult to make
            —Need pressing device
         b. One part: one rigid pressing surface
            —Slow
            —Unreliable quality
            —Low, uneven pressure
            —Easy to make
            —No press needed
   B. Application
      1. Ask students to categorize the molds
      2. Ask for an advantage or disadvantage of each form
      3. Exercises
         a. Describe molds
            —Matched molds
            —Ring molds
            —Gallon jar molds
            —Detergent bottle molds
         b. Divide into pairs
         c. Assign molds to pairs
         d. Follow instructions carefully
         e. Go to benches and begin

III. Follow-up
   A. What two kinds of molds did we use?
   B. Which is easier to use?
   C. Which is faster?
   D. Which is easier to make?
   E. Which do you suppose makes higher quality parts?

LESSON PLAN—*Questioning*

UNIT _____ Parts of Speech _____

LESSON TITLE _____ Defining Possessive Form of a Noun _____

OBJECTIVES   At the conclusion of this lesson, the student should be able, without references, to write a definition of the possessive form of a noun that is consistent with the lesson presentation.

REFERENCES

TEACHER ACTIVITY

Equipment

Materials

STUDENT ACTIVITY

Equipment

Materials

HO: Three Sentences

CONTENT AND PROCEDURES

I. I. Orientation: Aim
   A. Define *possessive form of noun* before using it
   B. Write a definition

II. Development
   A. Presentation
     1. Read "Three Sentences" (HO)
       a. The book belonging to the boy is on the table.
       b. The book of the boy is on the table.
       c. The boy's book is on the table.
     2. Think about what they are saying
     3. Do all three sentences have the same meaning?
     4. Which words in each sentence are exactly alike?
     5. Which words are different?
     6. Can one assume that the following are the same?
       a. "belonging to the boy"
       b. "of the boy"
       c. "boy's"
     7. If *boy's* is the possessive form, how can it be defined?
   B. Application: Individually write a definition of possessive form of a noun

III. Follow-up
   A. Randomly select students to read definitions
   B. Ask for commonalities
   C. Ask for differences
   D. Construct composite definition

LESSON PLAN–*Discussion*

UNIT _____ Writing Position Papers _____

LESSON TITLE _____ Defending Positions _____

OBJECTIVES   At the conclusion of this lesson, students should be able, when given a life and death situation, to clarify their values regarding people and their contributions to life on earth.

REFERENCES

Refer to the Project (Specific Skill) on pp. 86-87 for background.

TEACHER ACTIVITY

Equipment

Materials

STUDENT ACTIVITY

Equipment

Materials

CONTENT AND PROCEDURES

I. Orientation: How do you decide who lives or dies?

II. Development
    A. Presentation
        1. Values determine "an" answer
        2. We won't find "the" answer
    B. Application
        1. Let's discuss our "positions" on "who is saved in the plane crash" (details follow)
        2. Ask for volunteers (two to three)
        3. Tally or keep a record of each person saved
        4. Why was each person saved or left to perish?
        5. Would the decision be the same in
            a. India?
            b. England?
            c. Indian reservation?

III. Follow-up
    A. What values were used in making the decisions?

THE PLANE CRASH DILEMMA

1. Male, 72, on the verge of discovering cure for cancer
2. Female, 21, flying to meet her fiance
3. Male, 17, street gang leader, IQ of 180
4. Female, 5, emotionally withdrawn, has never spoken
5. Female, 18, unmarried, pregnant
6. Female, husband killed in Vietnam, has two children
7. Male, 42, minister involved in civil rights activities
8. Male, 58, alcoholic
9. Male, 17, voted "Most Likely to Succeed" in senior class
10. Female, 67, husband just died
11. Male, 36, ex-convict working in feed store, has three children
12. Female, 16, high school cheerleader
13. Female, 29, drug addict, has one child
14. Male, 12, physically handicapped
15. Female, 43, social worker
16. Male, 25, police officer
17. Female, 23, married to a 65-year-old millionaire
18. Female, 35, nurse in Vietnam
19. Male, 6, orphan
20. Female, 70, lives in old people's home
21. Your best friend
22. Your worst enemy
23. Male, 28, movie star
24. Male, 37, high school teacher
25. Male, 39, hijacker
26. Female, 21, Communist
27. Yourself

All of these people are on a crashing airplane—*only twelve can be saved.*
Which twelve would you save?

LESSON PLAN—*Buzz Session*

UNIT _____Early Civilization_____

LESSON TITLE _____Developing a Language_____

OBJECTIVES   At the conclusion of this lesson, the student should be able, when divided into groups of four to six, to—

1.   State three major problems of civilization and three solutions to each.
2.   Develop a new written language to replace our English language.
3.   When provided a copy of the language symbols, prove the efficiency of the language by translating a seventy-five-word paragraph in twenty minutes.

REFERENCES

TEACHER ACTIVITY

Equipment

Overhead projector

Materials

OT: Tools of the Time
OT: Picture This

STUDENT ACTIVITY

Equipment

Materials

Paper and pencils
HO: You Have Problems
        (basic problems)
HO: So You Think It's So
        Easy (developing a
        language)

CONTENT AND PROCEDURES

I. Orientation (HO: You Have Problems)
   A. Did other civilizations struggle as we do?
   B. Understand the complications of communication
   C. Test effective exchange

II. Development
   A. Presentation
      1. Problems of civilizations
         a. Shelter and safety
         b. Food
         c. Communication
      2. Solving Problems (OT: Tools of the Time)
         a. Tools and weapons
         b. Herding and agriculture
         c. Language
             —Verbal
             —Pictures (pictographs) (OT: Picture This)
             —Syllables (phonograms)
             —Alphabet (sound-sign)
      3. Improvement through exchange
         a. Within the family
         b. Within the community
         c. Civilization to civilization
             —Trade
             —Written
   B. Application
      1. Objectives (HO: So You Think It's So Easy)
         a. Circle three sentences from newspaper
         b. From circled sentences
             —Rewrite one as a *pictograph*
             —Rewrite one as a *phonogram*
         c. Develop a new language to replace English
         d. Write seventy-five words of circled story in new language
      2. Procedure
         a. Assemble into groups of four to six
         b. Identify leader to facilitate discussion
         c. Identify recorder to record and write final sentences, language, and paragraph
         d. Proceed

III. Follow-up
   A. Summary
      1. The problems of civilizations
      2. One solution to language—did we really communicate?
   B. Tasks for students
      1. List three major problems of humankind and 3 possible solutions within a ten-minute period
      2. Translate a new language paragraph into English in a twenty-minute period

LESSON PLAN—*Seminar*

UNIT _____ (Fits most subject areas) _____

LESSON TITLE _____ Planning a Seminar _____

OBJECTIVES   At the conclusion of this lesson, the student should be able, when asked at random, to—

1. Describe a seminar.
2. State one reason to conduct a seminar.
3. Describe how to plan a seminar.
4. State a student responsibility.
5. State the lead time needed to plan a seminar.

REFERENCES

TEACHER ACTIVITY

Equipment

Materials

STUDENT ACTIVITY

Equipment

Materials

HO: Seminar Agenda Items

CONTENT AND PROCEDURES

I. Orientation
    A.   Objectives
        1.   Describe the seminar technique
        2.   List the responsibilities
            a.   Teacher
            b.   Student
    B.   Tie-in—How we use seminars

II. Development
    A.   Presentation
        1.   What is a seminar?
        2.   Why have a seminar?
            a.   Group project
                —Coordinate efforts
                —Mutually support each other's efforts
                —Solve problems
            b.   Individual project
                —Report progress
                —Report findings
                —Report conclusions
                —Share results of project
                —Solve problems
        3.   How are seminars conducted?
            a.   Student-planned
                —Schedule
                —Agenda
                —Arrangements
            b.   Student-directed
            c.   Agenda items (HO: Seminar Agenda Items)
    B.   Application
        1.   Conducting a seminar is optional but recommended
        2.   Decide one week before seminar
        3.   Responsibilities
            a.   Schedule
            b.   Set and duplicate agenda
            c.   Contact any guests
            d.   Arrange room

III. Follow-up
    A.   What is a seminar?
    B.   Why conduct a seminar?
    C.   How is it planned?
    D.   What are student responsibilities?
    E.   How much lead time is needed?

LESSON PLAN—*Interviewing*

UNIT _____ Describing Careers _____

LESSON TITLE ___ Gathering Information _____

OBJECTIVES   At the conclusion of this lesson, the student should be able to—

1.   Select a suitable interviewee.
2.   Adequately prepare for the interview.
3.   Conduct an informative interview.
4.   Prepare a legible and comprehensive report of 200-500 words and hand it in on time.

REFERENCES

TEACHER ACTIVITY

Equipment

Materials

STUDENT ACTIVITY

Equipment

Materials

HO: Characteristics of Careers

CONTENT AND PROCEDURES

I. Orientation
    A. Why an interview?
        1. Effective source of information
        2. Consult experienced persons
        3. Consult knowledgeable persons
        4. Current
    B. Find out about a career related to the subject area

II. Development
    A. Presentation
        1. Prepare questions
            a. Information about occupation (HO: Characteristics of Careers)
              —General duties
              —Working conditions
              —Rewards
              —Preparation
              —Personal requirements
              —Levels within occupation
            b. Kinds of questions
              —Avoid one-word answers
              —Use *why* and *how*
              —Ask specialist to "describe. . ."
        2. Procedures
            a. Select interviewee carefully
            b. Take list of questions
            c. ·Take notes on answers
            d. Prepare 200-500-word report
              —Include each point under II.A.1.a.
              —Be legible
              —Due one week from today
    B. Application
        1. Ask teacher questions about teaching
            a. Duties
            b. Working conditions
            c. Rewards
            d. Preparation
            e. Personal requirements
            f. Levels of employment
        2. Discuss questions
            a. Which questions provided most information?
            b. How might information be summarized?
            c. Select interviewee

III. Follow-up
    A. What areas should questions be asked about?
    B. What kinds of questions are best?
    C. Whom should you interview?
    D. What procedures should you follow?
    E. Describe your report.

LESSON PLAN—*Role-Playing*

UNIT _____ Interaction Techniques _____

LESSON TITLE _____ "Bedtime Discipline" _____

OBJECTIVES   At the conclusion of this lesson, the student should be able, when given the role-playing situation on bedtime discipline, to state in writing within a 55-minute period five methods of dealing with a "procrastinating child."

REFERENCES

TEACHER ACTIVITY

Equipment

Overhead projector

Materials

OT: Role-Playing: What Is It?
OT: Audience Participation
OT: Blank Transparency
OT: Overhead Transparency Pens

STUDENT ACTIVITY

Equipment

Materials

HO: Role Descriptions

CONTENT AND PROCEDURES

I. Orientation
   A. Role-playing
      1. What is role-playing?
      2. Why use it?
         a. Experiment with new points of view
         b. Discover new interpretations
         c. Clarify values and goals
      3. We are using it for all reasons
   B. Rules
      1. No one ridiculed
      2. May make mistakes, so don't worry
      3. No one plays himself/herself

II. Development
   A. Presentation
      1. The situation
         a. Pass out roles (see handout: Role Descriptions)
           —Father
           —Mother
           —Three-year-old child
      2. Cast roles
         a. One student for each role
         b. Ask for volunteers
      3. Brief actors and audience
         a. Actors read their role characteristics
         b. Divide audience into the following "experts"
           (OT: Audience Participation)
           —Expert listeners
           —Expert watchers
           —Expert empathizers
           —Expert child consultants
   B. Application
      1. Begin interaction: speak for parents
         a. Experiencing difficulty getting child to bed
         b. Want to handle properly so this won't become an
           every night occurrence
      2. Stop interaction
         a. Reverse roles if necessary
         b. Allow "experts" to express views

III. Follow-up
   A. Class writes five constructive ways of dealing with "balky" child
      at bedtime
   B. Discuss the five methods
   C. Clarify values of methods in order of importance

ROLE DESCRIPTIONS

Father

Characteristics:

1. Wants time to unwind from work
2. Wants time to be alone with spouse
3. Needs time to work on a special project
4. May want to enjoy an evening television program
5. Wants to be firm but fair with child

Mother

Characteristics:

1. Needs time away from child
2. Wants to enjoy adult companionship
3. Tired from a full day of mothering
4. Worried about child's needed amount of sleep
5. Worried this situation will become a habit

Three-year-old child

Characteristics:

1. Afraid of the dark bedroom
2. Hears television, is curious about it and about what parents are doing
3. Tired but too wound up and not ready for sleep
4. Wants someone in the room

LESSON PLAN—*Gaming*

UNIT _____(Any subject matter is suitable)_____

LESSON TITLE _____Playing a Football Game_____

OBJECTIVES   At the conclusion of this lesson, students should be able to—

    1.   Practice for the game.
    2.   Play the game by:
            a.   Setting up the game
            b.   Following game rules
            c.   Putting game away.
    3.   Pass the final with a score of 85% or higher.
    4.   Enjoy themselves.

REFERENCES

TEACHER ACTIVITY

Equipment

Materials

STUDENT ACTIVITY

Equipment

Materials

   G: 1 for each two teams—Football Game
  HO: Football Game Rules

CONTENT AND PROCEDURES

I. Orientation—Purposes
 A. Prepare for final on _____
 B. Enjoy themselves

II. Development *(prior to game)*
 A. Presentation
  1. Identify teams
   a. Number off in 1's, 2's, 3's, and 4's
   b. Four to six per team
  2. Prepare for game
   a. What do teams do before the big game? (practice)
   b. What do they practice?
    —Rules
    —Study the subject
  3. Game schedule
   a. Three practice days
   b. Game one day prior to final
 B. Application
  1. Get teams together
  2. Plan practice sessions

III. Development *(on game day)*
 A. Presentation
  1. Review rules (HO: Football Game Rules)
  2. Teacher's role
   a. Referee
   b. Timekeeper
   c. Spectator
   d. Cheerleader
  3. End game five minutes before period ends
 B. Application
  1. Distribute games—one to each two teams
  2. Arrange students
   a. Opposing teams facing each other
   b. Table between
  3. Begin game

IV. Follow-up
 A. End game
 B. Determine winners
 C. Put games away
 D. Final exam

FOOTBALL GAME
RULES AND INSTRUCTIONS

The game may be played by each team on individual boards marked as football fields, or the field(s) may be drawn on the chalkboard with a student or the teacher marking the plays.

1. *Teams*

   At least two teams are needed. Teams with four members each are recommended. Before the game begins, identify the following members of each team:
   a. Captain
   b. Kickoff return player
   c. Punter
   d. Field goal kicker
   e. Order for answering questions.

2. *To Start*

   A toss of the coin determines the offensive and defensive teams. One team captain tosses the coin while the other calls it in the air. If the latter calls it correctly, his/her team receives. If not, his/her team kicks off.

3. *Kickoff* (four-item-listing questions)

   To kickoff, the defensive team captain takes the top card from the combined pile of Kickoff and Punt Questions and reads it to the offensive team's kickoff return player. This player's answer results in one of the following possibilities:

   a. If the kickoff return player provides all four answers correctly, there is a runback of twenty yards beyond his/her team's 20-yard line.

   b. If three answers are correct, there is a runback of fifteen yards beyond the 20-yard line.

   c. If two answers are correct, there is a runback of ten yards beyond the 20-yard line.

   d. If one answer is correct, there is a runback of five yards beyond the 20-yard line.

   e. If no answer is correct, there is no runback and the ball is placed on the 20-yard line.

4. *First Downs* (multiple choice or fill-in questions)

   Each Down Question is presented to a different member of the offensive team in the order decided upon before the game began. Down Questions can be asked by either the captain or individual team members. For each correct answer, advance the ball four yards.

   Three Down Questions must be answered correctly in order to earn a first down. First downs are followed by another series of three questions. When a Down Question is missed, the offensive player draws a Chance Card from a separate pile and follows the directions. (These cards contain negative directions or penalties.) If one or more Down Questions are missed, the offense must punt to the defense.

5. *Punts* (four-item-listing questions)

The Punt Question is read to the punter. The following possibilities are available:

a. If all four parts are correctly answered, the ball is advanced forty yards.

b. If three parts are correctly answered, the ball is advanced thirty yards.

c. If two parts are correctly answered, the ball is advanced twenty yards.

d. If one part is correctly answered, the ball is advanced ten yards.

e. If no part is correctly answered, the punt was blocked and the defense recovers on the line of scrimmage. After the punt, the defense takes over the ball.

6. *Touchdowns*

Touchdowns are made when the offense advances the ball to or beyond the goal line. Six (6) points are awarded for a touchdown.

7. *Extra Points* (true/false questions)

Extra Point Questions are presented to the next team member in the established order. One (1) point is awarded if the correct answer is given. After the extra point attempt, the offense kicks off to the other team.

8. *Field Goals* (three-item-listing questions)

If the offense has advanced the ball to or beyond the opponent's 30-yard line, *and* if one or more Down Questions were missed, a field goal can be attempted on fourth down. Questions from the Field Goal pile are used. All three answers must be correct to score a field goal. Three (3) points are awarded for a successful attempt. If any part of the question is missed, the defense gets the ball on its 20-yard line. When the offense is successful, the team kicks off to the other team.

9. *Ending the Game*

After a predetermined time *or* after Down Questions are used, the game ends.

SELECTED REFERENCES

SELECTED REFERENCES

ABLE Model Program. *Career Education Activities Through World of Work Resources.* DeKalb, Ill.: Northern Illinois University, 1972.

Bloom, Benjamin, S., ed. *Taxonomy of Educational Objectives. Handbook I: Cognitive Domain*. New York: David McKay Co., 1956.

Blount, Nathan S., and Klausmeir, Herbert J. *Teaching in the Secondary School.* Evanston, Ill.: Harper and Row, 1968.

Brown, James W.; Lewis, Richard B.; and Harcleroad, Fred F. *Audio-Visual Instruction: Technology, Media, and Methods*. 4th ed. New York: McGraw-Hill Book Co., 1973.

Callahan, Joseph F., and Clark, Leonard H. *Teaching in the Secondary School.* New York: Macmillan, 1977.

Clark, Leonard H. *Strategies and Tactics in Secondary School Teaching.* New York: Macmillan, 1968.

Colman, John E. *The Master Teachers and the Art of Teaching*. New York: Pitman Publishing Corp., 1967.

E.S.C. *Twenty-four Group Methods and Techniques in Adult Education.* Washington, D.C.: E.S.C., 1970.

Edwards, Clifford H., et al. *Planning, Teaching and Evaluation: A Competency Approach.* Chicago: Nelson-Hall, 1977.

Flanders, N. A. "Personal-Social Anxiety as a Factor in Experimental Learning Situations." *Journal of Educational Research* 45:100-110; October 1951.

Hamachek, Don E. *Motivation in Teaching and Learning*. Washington, D.C.: National Education Association, 1968.

Hauenstein, Dean A. *Curriculum Planning for Behavioral Development.* Worthington, Ohio: Charles A. Jones Publishing Co., 1972.

Henak, Dick. *Self-Teacher Education Packets.* Muncie, Ind.: Ball State University, 1974.

Jefferies, Derwin J. *Lesson Planning and Lesson Teaching.* Titusville, N.J.: Home and School Press, 1966.

Johnson, David W., and Johnson, Roger T. *Learning Together and Alone: Cooperation, Competition, and Individualization*. Englewood Cliffs, N.J.: Prentice-Hall, 1975.

Kilpatrick, William H. *Foundations of Method.* New York: Macmillan, 1930

Krathwohl, David R. *Taxonomy of Educational Objectives: Affective Domain.* New York: David McKay Co., 1964.

Leonard, Joan M.; Fallon, John J.; and von Arx, Harold. *General Methods of Effective Teaching.* New York: Thomas Y. Crowell., 1972.

Maley, Donald A. *The Industrial Arts Teacher's Handbook.* Boston: Allyn and Bacon, 1978.

_____. *The Maryland Plan.* New York: Bruce, 1973.

Means, Richard K. *Methodology in Education.* Columbus, Ohio: Charles E. Merrill Publishing Co., 1968.

Miller, W. R., and Rose, H. C. *Instructors and Their Jobs.* Chicago: American Technical Society, 1975.

Pierce, Walter D., and Forbes, Michael A. *Objectives and Methods for Secondary Teaching.* Englewood Cliffs, N.J.: Prentice-Hall, 1977.

Sanders, Norris M. *Classroom Questions: What Kinds?* New York: Harper and Row, 1966.